WHERE ON EARTH?
DINOSAURS
AND OTHER PREHISTORIC LIFE

Written by Chris Barker and Darren Naish
Consultant Darren Naish

Penguin Random House

Senior editor Ashwin Khurana
Senior art editors Rachael Grady, Stefan Podhorodecki
US editor Kayla Dugger **US executive editor** Lori Hand
Senior cartographic editor Simon Mumford
Editors Ann Baggaley, Chris Hawkes, Sarah MacLeod
Designers Chrissy Barnard, David Ball, Angela Ball
Illustrators James Kuether, Adam Benton,
Stuart Jackson-Carter, Peter Minister, Simon Mumford
Creative retouching Steve Crozier, Stefan Podhorodecki
Paleogeography maps Colorado Plateau Geosystems Inc

Jacket editor Emma Dawson **Jacket designer** Surabhi Wadha
Jacket design development manager Sophia MTT
Picture researcher Deepak Negi
Senior producer, pre-production Andy Hilliard
Senior producer Mary Slater

Managing editor Francesca Baines
Managing art editor Philip Letsu
Publisher Andrew Macintyre
Associate publishing director Liz Wheeler
Art director Karen Self
Design director Phil Ormerod
Publishing director Jonathan Metcalf

First American Edition, 2019
Published in the United States by DK Publishing
1450 Broadway, 8th floor, New York, NY 10018

A catalog record for this book is
available from the Library of Congress
ISBN 978-1-4654-7963-1

Printed and bound in Malaysia

A WORLD OF IDEAS:
SEE ALL THERE IS TO KNOW
www.dk.com

Smithsonian

Established in 1846, the Smithsonian—the world's largest museum,
education, and research complex—includes 19 museums and
galleries and the National Zoological Park. The total number of
artifacts, works of art, and specimens in the Smithsonian's collection
is estimated at 154 million. The Smithsonian is the world's largest
museum and research complex, dedicated to public education,
national service, and scholarship in the arts, sciences, and history.

CONTENTS

Yutyrannus

Rise of the dinosaurs

North America

Coelophysis

South America

Africa

Australia and Antarctica

Europe

Asia

After the dinosaurs

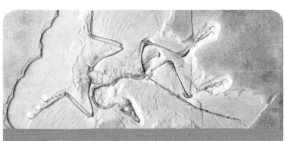

Reference

Polacanthus

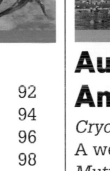

Hatzegopteryx

Giraffatitan

Foreword

My adventures as a paleontologist have taken me to many exciting places at home, in the UK, and abroad, and led to the discovery of new species. Working with teams of colleagues, I named the new dinosaurs *Eotyrannus*, *Xenoposeidon*, and *Mirischia*, and the pterosaurs *Vectidraco* and *Eurazhdarcho*. One of the things that interests me most about dinosaurs, giant marine reptiles, and other ancient animals is that every one of them has a unique history, just as animals do today.

In this book, you'll meet a huge variety of creatures that lived on our planet in the prehistoric past, mostly during the "age of the dinosaurs," around 235–66 million years ago. The stories about them here focus on where animals once lived and what this can tell us about them. Wild animals today live in specific areas, known as "ranges," which provide them with what they need to survive. Imagine a forest-dwelling, fruit-eating animal such as an orangutan. It cannot live anywhere but in a forest, and that must be a forest with the right kind of fruit trees. Some animals still live in the lands of their ancestors, while others have broadened their range, driven by factors such as climate and the slow shift of continents. In some cases, animals can discover new habitats by swimming or flying.

How our planet changed over millions of years, and how animals adapted to those changes, are exciting ideas. Exploring them will help us to picture prehistoric species as

the living
animals they once
were. Using the latest
and most up-to-date maps, this
book shows the ranges ancient animals
might have had, and what the world looked
like when they were alive. In many cases,
our knowledge is incomplete, and the true
ranges of these animals have yet to be
properly discovered.

I hope that this book inspires you to be interested
in Earth's fascinating prehistoric past and perhaps
to make scientific discoveries yourself if you're
lucky enough to have the opportunity.

Dr. Darren Naish

Understanding the locator globes

Earth's landmasses have changed over time, so
alongside every main map showing when and where
the prehistoric animal lived, you will also find a globe
to show you this area relative to modern-day Earth.

The first layer is the modern-day map of Earth,
outlining three major oceans.

This second, light-green layer shows what Earth's landmass would
have looked like when the profiled animal lived.

The third, dark-green layer represents the specific region shown
in the larger map featured on the pages.

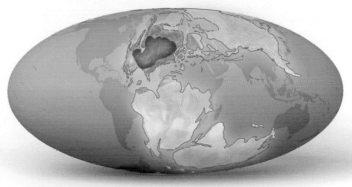

The final layer in red locates the roaming range of the profiled
animal, as reflected on the larger map.

RISE OF THE DINOSAURS

Triassic encounter
Alarmed by the appearance of the fearsome meat-eating reptile *Postosuchus*, a group of *Coelophysis* scurry frantically around. Another reptile, *Desmatosuchus*, moves wisely in the other direction.

Hominids

A group of primates appear, leading to the evolution of the great apes and, eventually, humans.

Dinosaurs

Dinosaurs appear in the Late Triassic, 235 million years ago, following a mass extinction at the end of the Permian.

Mammals

The ancestors of modern mammals evolve over 320 million years ago.

woolly mammoth

Land plants

The first plants appear on land in the Ordovician, at least 450 million years ago.

Animals

Around 600 million years ago, ancient animals such as sponges first appear, leaving behind occasional traces in the fossil record.

Timeline of Earth

Earth is old—4.6 billion years old, in fact. Yet estimates suggest our planet formed relatively rapidly, within only 10–20 million years. Rocks and metals floating in our Solar System began clumping together to form a large object spinning around an early Sun. Denser metals sank to the hot middle of the tough, rocky sphere to become Earth's core, while lighter rocks formed a crust, shaping Earth as we know it.

TODAY

PALEOZOIC

MESOZOIC

CENOZOIC

PROTEROZOIC

12

11

10

9

8

7

6

Multicellular life

Some eukaryotes evolve into multicellular life forms; these are the ancestors of plants, fungi, and animals.

Eukaryotes

Eurkaryotes, which are more complex life forms than prokaryotes, evolve over two billion years ago.

8

Earth over time

Some scientists describe the formation of Earth in terms of a 12-hour clock. This makes it easier to understand the scale and huge leaps of geological time. The clock starts at midnight, with the formation of Earth, with each hour representing roughly 375 million years. Some periods last several hours, and others barely a second.

Prokaryotes
The first forms of life evolve over 3.5 billion years ago, as simple single-celled organisms.

Geological time		Begins	Ends	Major events
Hadean		00:00:00	01:33:55	Unicellular life appears
Archean		01:33:55	05:28:41	Photosynthesis begins around 2:45 a.m.
Proterozoic		05:28:41	10:35:18	First eukaryotes appear around 6:30 a.m.; first multicellular life appears around 8.45 a.m.
PALEOZOIC	Cambrian	10:35:18	10:44:01	The Cambrian Explosion happens at 10:30 a.m.
	Ordovician	10:44:01	10:50:31	Mollusks and arthropods dominate the seas
	Silurian	10:50:31	10:54:22	First land plants appear
	Devonian	10:54:22	11:03:49	The age of bony fishes
	Carboniferous	11:03:49	11:13:12	Large coal deposits formed from vast swamp forests; amphibians and insects invade the land
	Permian	11:13:12	11:20:34	Rise of the reptiles
MESOZOIC	Triassic	11:20:34	11:28:30	The first dinosaurs
	Jurassic	11:28:30	11:37:18	Dinosaurs dominate
	Cretaceous	11:37:18	11:49:40	Dinosaur extinction
CENOZOIC	Paleocene	11:49:40	11:51:14	Mammals begin to dominate
	Eocene	11:51:14	11:54:42	Warm, wet climate; modern mammal families arise
	Oligocene	11:54:42	11:56:24	Dry, cool climate; continents are nearing current positions
	Miocene	11:56:24	11:59:10	Hominids (early human ancestors) appear
	Pliocene	11:59:10	11:59:36	Temperatures (on Earth) cool
	Pleistocene	11:59:36	11:59:49	Major ice ages occur
	Holocene	11:59:49	12:00:00	Modern humans appear

Baryonyx

Ankylosaurus

9

Early life

The origins of life are shrouded in mystery. Evidence suggests that it evolved roughly half a billion years after Earth's creation.

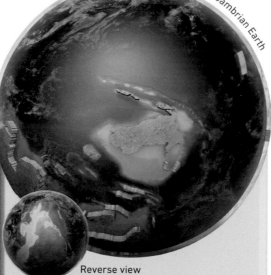

Cambrian Earth

Ordovician Earth

Reverse view

STEPPING STONES TO LIFE

The development of life was probably a gradual, multistep process, as molecules (groups of atoms) assembled and developed a structure and the ability to reproduce themselves. Some scientists have suggested life originated in the deep sea, in vents near volcanoes that spew hot, chemical-rich water.

Life appears
Four billion years ago in the Hadean, organisms made of a single cell, called prokaryotes, were the first life forms to appear.

Sun power
Around 3.5 billion years ago during the Archean, early organisms began producing energy from the Sun's light—a process we know today as photosynthesis.

Eukaryotes
Complex, single-celled organisms, called eukaryotes, evolved more than 2 billion years ago in the Proterozoic.

Multicellular life
Around 1.7 billion years ago in the Proterozoic, some eukaryotes became multicellular organisms. These are the ancestors of plants and animals.

Reverse view

CAMBRIAN PERIOD (541–485 MYA)

The Cambrian Explosion occurred 541 million years ago and refers to the huge and rapid diversification of life that saw most of the modern animal groups emerge. These animals began developing new lifestyles, with many swimming or burrowing in the ancient oceans. Features such as eyes also evolved for the first time.

PLANET EARTH
A global supercontinent, known as Pannotia, was breaking up into smaller plates. Fluctuating sea levels led to a succession of "ice ages."

TYPES OF LIFE
Animals: Many ocean-dwelling invertebrate animals were successful, including arthropods and mollusks.
Plants: Plants had yet to evolve.

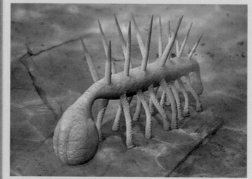

Hallucigenia is now extinct

ORDOVICIAN PERIOD (485–443 MYA)

Arthropods and mollusks continued to thrive during the Ordovician, while new types of fish also evolved. However, by the end of this period, a mass extinction—possibly caused by cooling temperatures—wiped out many marine habitats.

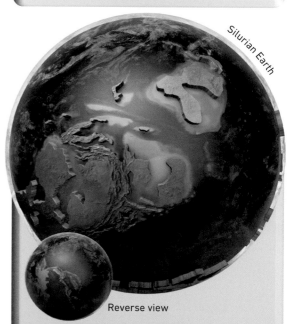

Silurian Earth

Reverse view

SILURIAN PERIOD (443–419 MYA)

Fish continued to diversify after the extinction event, sharing a habitat with giant sea scorpions. On land, early plants developed tissue with the ability to transport water and began to colonize areas next to lakes and streams.

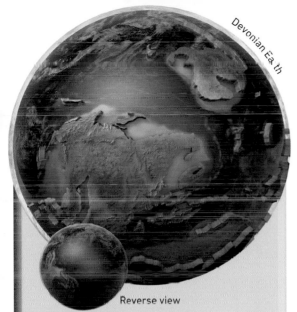

Reverse view

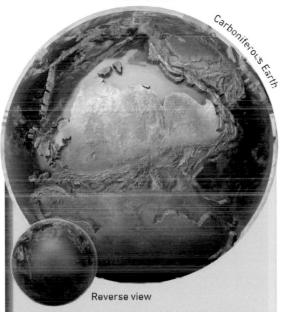

Reverse view

Reverse view

DEVONIAN PERIOD (419–358 MYA)

The "Age of Fishes" took place during the Devonian, with species evolving into many different shapes and sizes. The placoderms were the top predators—huge, armored fish with bone-crunching bites. However, these creatures would not survive at the end of this period.

PLANET EARTH
The supercontinent Gondwana made up much of the Southern Hemisphere and was starting to collide with the continent of Euramerica. This was the start of the creation of the supercontinent known as Pangea.

TYPES OF LIFE
Animals: The first insects explored the land. Meanwhile, fish such as *Tiktaalik* began showing features seen in later four-legged semi-aquatic animals such as *Acanthostega*.

Tiktaalik

Plants: Moss forests and plants with primitive roots began to take hold of the land, and by the Late Devonian, the oldest-known trees had emerged.

Impression of extinct *Archaeopteris* trees

CARBONIFEROUS PERIOD (358–298 MYA)

The invasion of the land took hold during the Carboniferous, creating lush forests teeming with wildlife. These forests grew so quickly that billions of tons of their remains were buried, forming the coal we use today. Insects also grew huge due to the air's high oxygen levels.

PLANET EARTH
Pangea had formed by the Carboniferous, with all but a few Asian subcontinents colliding to form the giant landmass. In the south, ice sheets spread across several places by the end of the period.

TYPES OF LIFE
Animals: Sharks thrived in the sea, while giant arthropods, some up to 6.5 ft (2 m) long, patrolled the land. Amphibians, such as *Amphibamus*, were now diverse and common, while the

Amphibamus

first reptiles also evolved, looking very similar to the lizards of today. Reptiles would continue to diversify throughout the period.

Plants: Huge, dense forests, some filled with plants that reached as tall as 98 ft (30 m), covered large parts of Carboniferous Pangea.

Carboniferous forests resembled this modern swamp

PERMIAN PERIOD (298–252 MYA)

The Carboniferous Rainforest Collapse at the end of the previous era left behind huge, dry, desertlike areas. These harsher conditions meant amphibians were no longer as widespread. Reptiles, on the other hand, were better adapted to the arid environment.

PLANET EARTH
All the continents had collided to form Pangea. The period inherited an ice age from the Carboniferous, but became gradually warmer and drier.

TYPES OF LIFE
Animals: Both reptiles and a group of animals called synapsids (right) dominated much of the food chain, and included large herbivores and carnivores. However, these would be severely affected by the huge mass extinction at the end of the period, probably caused by the release of volcanic gases.

Lystrosaurus

Plants: Seed-producing plants such as conifers and cycads made up much of the plant life.

Artwork of the End Permian extinction event

Triassic world

252–201 MYA

Throughout much of the Triassic, life on Earth was still recovering from the devastating mass extinction at the end of the Permian. It was not until the Late Triassic that the first dinosaurs began to evolve, living on a single vast supercontinent known as Pangea.

Reverse view

Planet Earth

At this time, the land formed a single vast continent known as Pangea, which began splitting apart in the Late Triassic.

Long reach
The long neck of *Plateosaurus* allowed the animal to reach tall plants, which it cut up with its leaf-shaped back teeth.

Early dinosaur battle
In this Late Triassic depiction, a small group of hungry young *Liliensternus* attempt to bring down a *Plateosaurus* much larger than themselves. Despite their advantage in numbers, this is a risky venture for the predators.

Environment

The shape of the continent affected the global climate, making life during the Triassic very different from modern times.

CLIMATE
The average Triassic temperature was about 62.6°F (17°C)—with the interior of Pangea receiving hardly any rain. However, the oceans kept life on the coasts cooler and wetter.

PLANTS
Many plants took a long time to recover from the Permian mass extinction, but ferns, ginkgos, and conifers survived. Flowering plants had not yet evolved.

Fern

Animals

Lacking competitors, the survivors of the mass extinction were briefly successful. However, new animal groups began to evolve, some of which would dominate Earth for millions of years.

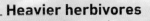
Fossil cockroach

INVERTEBRATES
Insects began to develop into a much larger range of species throughout the Triassic. They included cockroaches, flies, and aquatic species. In the sea, modern, stony corals began to appear.

FIRST DINOSAURS
During the Late Triassic, approximately 235 million years ago, the first dinosaurs evolved. They were small, carnivorous creatures that ran around on two legs.

OTHER LAND REPTILES
Predatory relatives of modern crocodiles and alligators sat at the top of the food chain. Turtles also began to evolve, while pterosaurs took to the sky.

Mixosaurus, a small ichthyosaur

MARINE REPTILES
A diverse range of marine reptiles evolved in the Triassic, including ichthyosaurs, plesiosaurs, nothosaurs, and shell-crushing placodonts. Some, such as the nothosaurs and placodonts, would die out at the end of the Triassic, while others continued to prosper in the Mesozoic seas.

Proganochelys turtles date from the Triassic

Heavier herbivores
The first large plant-eating dinosaurs, such as this *Plateosaurus,* belonged to a group called sauropodomorphs. These animals moved on two legs.

Larger predators
By the Late Triassic, bigger 16-ft (5-m) long theropods such as *Liliensternus* began to evolve, These dinosaurs were capable of attacking large prey.

Jurassic world

201–145 MYA

As the supercontinent of Pangea split into two separate landmasses—Laurasia and Gondwana—both climate and life on Earth changed. With longer coastlines creating more moisture and warm, humid conditions, plants spread fast and new species developed in lush environments. Dinosaurs dominated on land and grew even bigger.

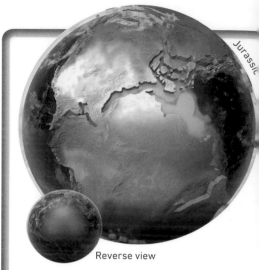

Reverse view

Planet Earth

The Atlantic Ocean began to appear, as the moving continents and the advancing Tethys Ocean slowly separated North America from Africa.

Killer alert

In this Early Jurassic landscape, a pair of predatory *Dilophosaurus* watch as a third one comes down to the water to drink. The appearance of these large carnivores has made the long-necked *Sarahsaurus* nervous.

Crested snout

The double crest rising from the snout of *Dilophosaurus* is thought to have been used for display.

Top fliers

Although birds appeared during the Jurassic, pterosaurs such as *Rhamphinion* still dominated the skies.

Environment

A mass extinction at the end of the Triassic allowed dinosaurs to flourish, while the increasing coastlines brought climate change.

CLIMATE

With a warm climate averaging 61.7°F (16.5°C), there were no ice caps at the poles. An increase in coastlines produced more moisture in the air, which fell as rain, creating humid habitats perfect for plants. All these plants increased oxygen levels in the air.

PLANTS

Jurassic Earth still had no flowering plants and was instead dominated by forests of conifers and ginkgos, as well as by ferns and cycads. This plant life sustained the large herbivorous dinosaurs.

Cycad

Animals

With many Triassic reptiles now extinct, the dinosaurs took over, introducing new lifestyles. The number of dinosaur species grew rapidly, with many variations in size and shape.

MARINE ANIMALS

Invertebrates such as ammonites and belemnites, cousins of modern-day octopuses and squids, flourished in the warm Jurassic seas.

LAND INVERTEBRATES

Insects thrived in the forests, the smaller ones surviving the arrival of new predators—birds—better than the larger ones.

GIANT DINOSAURS

Armored stegosaurs and large theropods were weighing in at the multiton mark, but it was the sauropods that became truly huge.

MARINE REPTILES

Ichthyosaurs, plesiosaurs, and crocodilian relatives, such as toothy *Dakosaurus*, hunted in the oceans.

LAND ANIMALS

The first birds appeared during the Jurassic, evolving from a branch of theropods. Lizards scurried around in the undergrowth. Early mammal relatives also evolved, but they would remain in the shadow of dinosaurs for a long time to come.

Dakosaurus

Cylindroteuthis

Triassic relic
The small *Coelophysis*, one of the earliest-known theropods, may have survived into the Jurassic.

Synapsids
Small animals belonging to a group known as synapsids lived in the Jurassic. They are the relatives of modern mammals.

Cretaceous world

145–66 MYA

By the end of the Cretaceous, drifting landmasses had split up into the continents we see today. Dinosaurs remained the dominant large animals on land, while new bird and mammal species evolved. However, an 8.7-mile (14-km) wide asteroid would collide with Earth, closing this period with a mass extinction that wiped out 75 percent of all species.

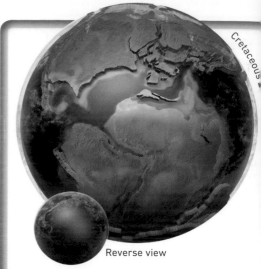

Reverse view

Planet Earth
During the Cretaceous, the expanding Atlantic Ocean pushed North America away from Africa, while Gondwana split into South America, Antarctica, and India.

Tyrant lizard
By the Late Cretaceous, tyrannosaurs such as *Lythronax* were the top carnivores of the northern hemisphere.

Environment

The fragmenting continents and high sea levels created a wide variety of new environments, which sped up the evolution of new species.

CLIMATE

The cooling temperatures of the Late Jurassic continued into the Cretaceous but soon rose again. The climate was generally warm for the remainder of the period, perhaps due to increased volcanic activity. The average temperature was 64.4°F (18°C).

PLANTS

Flowering plants evolved in the Cretaceous and rapidly spread across the globe. Grasses also evolved, but were not as widespread as today. Other plants seen throughout the Mesozoic, such as conifers and ferns, continued to thrive.

Flowering plant

Animals

The changing world saw animal life become more diverse as it took advantage of new habitats and food sources. The now separated continents isolated animals from one another and, as they learned to survive in different habitats, new species evolved.

Eomaia

LAND INVERTEBRATES

With the appearance of flowers, bees and other pollinating insects evolved to feed on the nectar.

MAMMALS

The relatives of modern mammals began to adopt different lifestyles, such as meat eating and semiaquatic foraging

DINOSAURS

Dinosaurs still ruled the land, with giant predators—including feathered theropods such as *Dakotaraptor*—and even bigger plant eaters. Birds became even more varied.

MARINE LIFE

Modern forms of marine life, such as sharks and bony fish, became common, and some reached huge sizes. Ichthyosaurs, however, became extinct by the Late Cretaceous and were replaced by mosasaurs.

Iberomesornis

Eating machines

Hadrosaurs developed rows of hundreds of densely stacked teeth, called dental batteries, that helped to grind down vegetation.

Watery habitat

The hadrosaurs *Adelolophus* and *Acristavus* keep an eye on the nearby tyrannosaur *Lythronax*. Two *Diabloceratops* continue to battle, unaware of the predator's arrival. Fossils of these Cretaceous dinosaurs, dated 82–79 million years ago, have been found in North America's Wahweap Formation.

What is a dinosaur?

Dinosaurs evolved from small reptiles about 235 million years ago. Based on the shape and structure of bones in the skull, neck, arm, hip, and ankle, this family tree shows the dinosaur groups. However, with exciting discoveries continually being made, this structure may change over time.

Saurischians

These are called "lizard-hipped" dinosaurs, though not all of them had hip bones like those of a lizard. They had long neck bones and often a large claw on each hand.

Coelophysis

Early relatives

The dinosaurs belong to a larger group of reptiles called dinosauriforms, which includes their closest relatives. These reptilian cousins first appeared 245 million years ago, but do not share all dinosaur traits.

Dinosaur cousin
The tiny Triassic reptile *Marasuchus* was related to the dinosaurs and looked like them in many ways, but was not a direct ancestor.

Psittacosaurus

Ornithischians

The "bird-hipped" ornithischian dinosaurs had backward-pointing hip bones similar to those of birds. They also had an extra bone, the predentary, in the lower jaw.

What is *not* a dinosaur?

The Mesozoic world was full of amazing reptiles that flourished both on land and in the ocean, but not all of them were dinosaurs. These other creatures, which are often confused with dinosaurs, include the marine reptiles, the crocodilians and their relatives, and flying pterosaurs.

Ocean-dwelling animal
This Late Jurassic ichthyosaur was a fast swimmer and fed on squid and fish.

Stenopterygius

Hatzegopteryx

Theropods

The dinosaurs that would eventually give rise to birds were bipedal—they walked on two legs. Many theropods were predators, but some ate plants.

Tyrannosaurus

Sauropodomorphs

Although early species were bipedal, most members of this group walked on four legs and had a distinctive long neck and tail. Some became gigantic.

Diplodocus

Pachycephalosaurs

These bipedal plant eaters had heads made for combat, with flattened or dome-shaped skulls up to 10 in (25 cm) thick. This feature helped to protect the brain from heavy blows.

Pachycephalosaurus

Ceratopsians

With some of the largest skulls of any land animal, the horned ceratopsians ranged from small bipeds to multiton quadrupeds.

Triceratops

Ornithopods

Some of these hugely successful herbivores had showy crests for display and hundreds of plant-crushing teeth.

Corythosaurus

Stegosaurs

With plates and spikes running down their backs and tails, and occasionally protruding from their shoulders, these large herbivores were excellent defenders.

Stegosaurus

Ankylosaurs

Wide bodies, various plates, spikes, and tail clubs armed the herbivorous ankylosaurs against predators.

Ankylosaurus

Cerapoda

Thyreophorans

Walking tall

Many dinosaurs evolved limbs that were set under the body to support their weight and allow them to walk upright.

The sprawling limbs of lizards do not support their weight, so their bellies touch the ground.

A crocodilian can lift its body in a "high walk" on straighter legs, but this uses a lot of energy.

All dinosaurs stood tall on straight legs and had a hinged ankle, so walking took less effort.

NORTH AMERICA

Muddy battle
Two *Allosaurus* take down a towering *Diplodocus*. Alongside some of the largest and most ferocious animals that ever lived, they roamed the continent now known as North America.

220 MYA

Supercontinent
At this time, all the continents were joined in a supercontinent called Pangea, enabling *Coelophysis* to travel across a lot of the globe.

PACIFIC OCEAN

ATLANTIC OCEAN

INDIAN OCEAN

P A N G E A

Up north
Many *Coelophysis* fossils have been found in North America.

Far and wide
Coelophysis also roamed modern-day South America and Africa. Their remains are often found in ancient floodplains.

Fragile arms
Although long, this dinosaur's arms were rather weak and weren't very useful for tackling big prey.

The inside truth
When bones were first found in the stomach of an adult *Coelophysis* specimen, experts thought this dinosaur was a cannibal. However, it turned out these bones were actually from a different reptile.

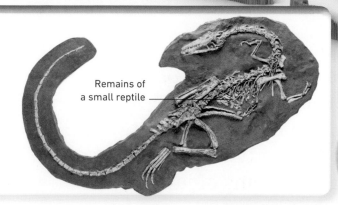

Remains of a small reptile

Open wide

The jaws of the long snout acted like scissors but had a relatively weak bite.

Body types

Experts initially identified two body types of *Coelophysis*, thought to be a male and a female. However, recent research suggests the difference between types is not based on sex.

Longer skull

Slender thighbone

"Gracile" body type
This type was 9.8 ft (3 m) long, with a slender body and more flexible backbones.

Thicker tail

"Robust" body type
Although the same size as the gracile body type, it weighed more, causing some scientists to argue this was the male.

Razor-sharp teeth

Fifty-three small, serrated teeth lined the jaws. These were perfect for catching prey, which it then swallowed whole.

Flexible neck

A long, bendy neck helped this dinosaur catch small reptiles and early mammals.

Coelophysis

SEE-low-FYE-sis

From modern-day North America to Africa, *Coelophysis* fossils are spread far and wide. This 3-ft (2-m) long dinosaur is also one of the earliest to roam the planet, living 220–190 million years ago. Over a thousand specimens have been identified, including the remains of juveniles.

Agile hunter

Coelophysis was a typical theropod—it walked on two legs, had an S-shaped neck, and had a long tail for balance. With excellent eyesight, it probably hunted small, agile prey.

AS MASSIVE, LAND-DWELLING RELATIVES OF TODAY'S CROCODILES.

EUROPE

Open woodland
Most dinosaurs, including *Stegosaurus*, lived near floodplains and areas of large, widely spaced trees.

PACIFIC OCEAN

ATLANTIC OCEAN

INDIAN OCEAN

NORTH AMERICA

Throat armor
Bony scales protected its throat.

Dry land
The arid climate in the southern regions of North America may not have provided enough food for *Stegosaurus*.

Flexible tail
The near 3.3-ft (1-m) long spikes on the bendy tail were probably used to ward off predators.

Stegosaurus

STEG-oh-SORE-us

Instantly recognizable with its spiked tail and plated back, the 29.5-ft (9-m) long, 6.5-ton *Stegosaurus* is one of the most famous Jurassic dinosaurs. It ate its way through much of North America and some parts of Europe.

Fossils in Portugal
At this time, Europe and North America were joined by a land bridge. In fact, *Stegosaurus* remains have been identified in Portugal.

Plated plant eater
Living 155–151 million years ago, *Stegosaurus* is perhaps best known for its dorsal plates. However, scientists still aren't certain what they were for. Some experts think they were for display, as they were too high on the body to be used for defense. Others argue the plates helped regulate its body temperature.

Decorative plates
Covered in keratin (material that forms birds' beaks), the plates might have been brightly colored.

Brainy myth
The 19th-century American paleontologist Othniel Charles Marsh thought that an expansion of the spinal cord near the hips of *Stegosaurus* housed a secondary brain. This is not true, and this space probably contained nerves that controlled muscular movement.

The site of the incorrectly proposed "hip brain."

A *Stegosaurus* brain was about the same size as a small dog's.

Three against one

Grazing in the Late Jurassic sun, a *Stegosaurus* finds itself cornered by three *Allosaurus*. The smaller plated dinosaur may be outnumbered, but its flexible, spiked tail can inflict deadly wounds. The outcome is far from certain.

Eye horns

Small horns above the eyes were perhaps used to attract mates.

150 MYA

Serrated teeth

Almost 80 teeth lined the jaws, perfect for slicing through flesh.

Open wide

Experts are uncertain of how *Allosaurus* bit its prey. It could open its mouth a massive 79 degrees and had a strongly built skull, yet the force of its bite was not exceptional. Some scientists believe it used its upper jaw like a hatchet to make long, slashing wounds.

Violent behavior

Marks on some *Allosaurus* fossils indicate rivalry with dangerous dinosaurs. One specimen in particular shows evidence of an aggressive infection in its hip bone, courtesy of a *Stegosaurus* spike puncturing the bone.

Allosaurus

al-oh-**SORE**-us

Averaging 30 ft (9 m) in length, this prime predator was a common theropod that patrolled much of North America and parts of Europe 156–144 million years ago. With its serrated teeth, large claws, and powerful leg muscles, this carnivore was built for the hunt.

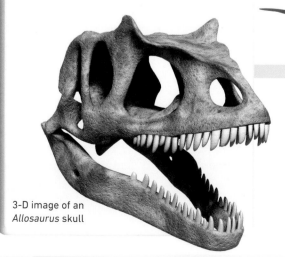

3-D image of an *Allosaurus* skull

ANALYSIS OF NECK MUSCLES SHOWED THAT *ALLOSAURUS*

EUROPE

PACIFIC
OCEAN

ATLANTIC
OCEAN

INDIAN
OCEAN

European range
Allosaurus, like other Late Jurassic dinosaurs, exploited the land bridge between North America and western Europe to colonize both continents.

Semiarid climate
Distinct wet and dry seasons shaped much of North America, with conifers and ferns exploiting the water around rivers.

Common predator
Allosaurus accounts for three-quarters of all theropod fossils found in the Jurassic rock layer called the Morrison Formation.

Dry south
Mountains to the west prevented rainfall from falling eastward, creating an arid climate in the south.

NORTH
AMERICA

Massive claws
Allosaurus had three hooked claws at the end of its fingers, the largest measuring 7 in (18 cm) long. Attached to powerful arms, these claws may have been effective in grabbing onto struggling prey or wrestling other *Allosaurus* during combat.

Counterbalance
The long tail helped to balance the front of the body, stabilizing *Allosaurus* on its two legs.

Sharp claws
Large, pointed claws could have been dangerous weapons.

Fossilized *Allosaurus* claw

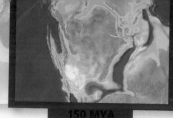
Strange horn
Ceratosaurus is Greek for "horn lizard."

Nose-y predator
Analysis of a *Ceratosaurus* brain reveals this dinosaur had a good sense of smell.

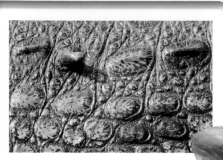

Bony skin

Ceratosaurus had osteoderms running down the middle of the neck, back, and tail. These are small bones embedded in the skin, similar to those seen in crocodiles today (above), and were perhaps used in display.

NORTH AMERICA

Toothy predator

This ferocious, toothy hunter roamed North America around 150–144 million years ago. *Ceratosaurus'* teeth were proportionally longer than those of other Jurassic predators. They helped it slice deeply into flesh, perfect for catching smaller herbivorous dinosaurs.

Fierce bite
Ceratosaurus could deliver fast, slashing bites.

Useful tail
The tall tail bones possibly helped this dinosaur to swim.

CERATOSAURUS

EUROPE

Wetland specialist
Unlike other bipedal dinosaurs of the time, *Ceratosaurus* were commonly found around water sources.

European dinosaurs
Bones have been found in Europe, supporting the idea that a land bridge once existed between the two continents.

PACIFIC OCEAN

ATLANTIC OCEAN

INDIAN OCEAN

Nasal horn
The 6-in (15-cm) tall horn that adorned *Ceratosaurus* is somewhat of a mystery. Juveniles had smaller horns, supporting the idea that this adaptation was used once they were old enough to compete for mating rights.

Early illustration of *Ceratosaurus* skull

Spiked and dangerous
Ceratosaurus was one of the few meat-eating dinosaurs to have small, bony scales covering the top of its body.

Ceratosaurus

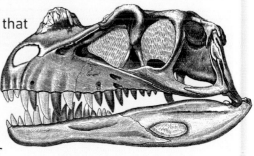

ser-**AT**-oh-**SORE**-us

Small arms
Probably too small for catching prey, this dinosaur's arms might have helped it to get up from the ground.

This rare Jurassic predator had to compete for food and space with larger dinosaurs, such as the more common *Allosaurus*. At a terrifying 23 ft (7 m) long, its most striking features were the horns above its eyes and snout.

WAS ONE OF THE RARE CARNIVOROUS DINOSAURS TO POSSESS HORNS.

Small head

Relative to its incredible size, the skull of *Diplodocus* was tiny—only 24 in (60 cm) long, or about the size of a horse's head. As a result, this dinosaur also had a small brain, which occupied a fist-sized cavity at the back of the skull.

Fossilized *Diplodocus* skull

Giant plant eater

With its long neck and whiplike tail, *Diplodocus* is easily recognizable. Yet, despite its size, this plant-eating dinosaur was relatively lightweight, weighing between 11 and 17 tons.

Peglike teeth

Diplodocus consumed up to 73 lb (33 kg) of leaves and ferns daily. Its hard-working teeth fell out and were replaced monthly.

Diplodocus

dip-**LOD**-oh-kuss

Growing to 108 ft (33 m) in length, *Diplodocus* was one of the longest dinosaurs that ever lived. This massive Jurassic herbivore marched throughout the area that is now North America 150–145 million years ago, searching for plants to help fuel its bulky body.

ONE ADULT *DIPLODOCUS* WOULD HAVE BEEN ABOUT THE

Sundance Sea
Extending some distance across North America, this body of water was formed by rivers draining from the nearby mountains. It does not exist today.

PACIFIC OCEAN

INDIAN OCEAN

Diverse plant life
Despite the dry climate, conifer trees, ginkgos, and tree ferns still managed to thrive in the Late Jurassic.

Dorsal spines
Some experts think that sharp, tough spines may have extended down the neck, back, and tail.

Arid climate
The tall mountains in western North America prevented much rain from falling toward the eastern regions. This created a savannahlike climate.

NORTH AMERICA

Flexible neck
This helped *Diplodocus* to feed over large areas without wasting a lot of energy walking.

Impressive tail
Made up of 80 bones, the tail may have lashed out at enemies.

Wetlands
These dinosaurs sometimes found sanctuary from predators in swamps, although they generally inhabited forested areas.

LARAMIDIA

Western Interior Seaway

Crested skull

The crest may have amplified low, deep calls produced by *Corythosaurus*. These calls might have been used to attract mates, show dominance, or warn of approaching predators.

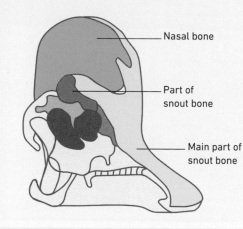

Nasal bone

Part of snout bone

Main part of snout bone

Forested areas
There was plenty of vegetation to feed all the hungry herbivores in lush, densely packed forests.

Corythosaurus

ko-**RITH**-oh-**SORE**-us

Big eyes
Good vision allowed it to see a far-off rival or mate.

Notable for the dramatic crest on its skull, *Corythosaurus* was a large, 30-ft (9-m) long duck-billed dinosaur, or hadrosaur. It lived in woodland and swamplike habitats about 77–74 million years ago, alongside various other large herbivores.

THE FIRST *CORYTHOSAURUS* SPECIMEN FOUND WAS SO WELL

Herbivore heaven

Many large herbivores lived at this time in North America, including other hadrosaurs. So it is likely that *Corythosaurus* specialized in eating specific plants, so as not to be in direct competition with these dinosaurs for food.

Narrow beak

Corythosaurus had a slimline beak that was adapted to a more selective feeding habit than other hadrosaurs.

Growing crest

Baby *Corythosaurus* were born without a crest. But, as this dinosaur grew, a crest gradually appeared and became larger with age.

Healthy diet

Conifer needles, seeds, and fruits have been found in the ribcage of one specimen. It would have fed on these just before it died.

ATLANTIC OCEAN

PACIFIC OCEAN

INDIAN OCEAN

PRESERVED, YOU COULD SEE TRACES OF ITS SKIN.

APPALACHIA

Western Interior Seaway

Appalachia
As the inland sea, called the Western Interior Seaway, shrank, the Appalachian landmass would meet Laramidia to form North America as we know it today.

Massive jaws
Within the 3-ft (1-m) long skull, more than 50 teeth lined the bone-crunching jaws of *Albertosaurus*. A fully grown adult could probably have targeted dangerous herbivores as large as itself.

Small "horns" above eyes

LARAMIDIA

Lush forests
Albertosaurus roamed the forests of modern-day Canada, where the first fossil of this dinosaur was found.

PACIFIC OCEAN

Albertosaurus
al-BERT-oh-SORE-us

At 30 ft (9 m) long, *Albertosaurus* was more lightly built than its later tyrannosaur cousins. Yet with its sharp teeth and excellent hunting skills, it rose to be a top predator in North America 74–70 million years ago.

Two claws
Small, two-clawed arms are typical of tyrannosaurs.

Feathery debate
Some experts argue that large tyrannosaurs such as *Albertosaurus* possessed feathers.

Predator poop
Scientists have found and studied fossilized tyrannosaur droppings to find out more about these predators. Being meat eaters, food passed through the gut very rapidly. Some droppings contained finely ground bone and even undigested muscle tissue.

Long legs
This leggy predator could easily travel long distances.

Dewclaw
The small first digit, or dewclaw, was set high on the leg and never touched the ground.

Sore jaw
Some *Albertosaurus* jawbones show holes that could have been caused by infection.

ATLANTIC OCEAN

PACIFIC OCEAN

INDIAN OCEAN

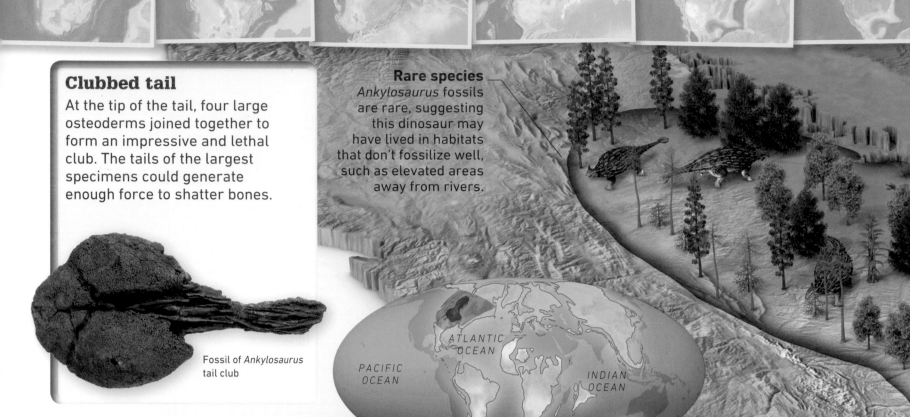

Clubbed tail

At the tip of the tail, four large osteoderms joined together to form an impressive and lethal club. The tails of the largest specimens could generate enough force to shatter bones.

Fossil of *Ankylosaurus* tail club

Rare species

Ankylosaurus fossils are rare, suggesting this dinosaur may have lived in habitats that don't fossilize well, such as elevated areas away from rivers.

ATLANTIC OCEAN

PACIFIC OCEAN

INDIAN OCEAN

NORTH AMERICA

Wide ribcage

This dinosaur's broad ribcage housed a long digestive system that broke down tough vegetation.

Ankylosaurus

ANK-ill-oh-SORE-us

Covered in armored skin and wielding a huge tail club, the 23-ft (7-m) long *Ankylosaurus* was a master of defense. Living in North America 74–66 million years ago, its heavy body and low center of gravity enabled it to survive in an environment dominated by the fearsome *Tyrannosaurus*.

ANKYLOSAURUS HAD A LARGE, MUSCULAR, AND FLEXIBLE TONGUE.

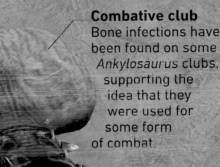

Combative club
Bone infections have been found on some *Ankylosaurus* clubs, supporting the idea that they were used for some form of combat.

Tough opponent
With its bones that grew in the skin and covered the neck, back, and tail—known as osteoderms—*Ankylosaurus* could withstand the toughest enemies. This plant eater's head was also incredibly strong, with bones fused together that increased the skull's strength, protecting the dinosaur's brain.

Drying sea
This dinosaur lived on the western shore of the Western Interior Seaway, which was rapidly drying up.

Bony plates
Hundreds of armor plates of various sizes protected the body of *Ankylosaurus*.

Nasal cavity
The complex airways on the snout are likely to have helped retain water and control body temperature.

King of the West

Living in forests and swamps, *Tyrannosaurus* dominated western North America. This mighty dinosaur had the ability to attack and kill almost anything that crossed its path.

NORTH AMERICA

ATLANTIC OCEAN

PACIFIC OCEAN

INDIAN OCEAN

PACIFIC OCEAN

Mexican remains

Tyrannosaurus-like remains have been found as far south as Mexico, although some researchers are still skeptical as to the identity of their owner.

Tyrannosaurus

TIE-ran-oh-SORE-us

The immense 40-ft (12-m) long body, powerful muscles, and fearsome reputation make *Tyrannosaurus* the most iconic dinosaur species. In fact, we now know more about its biology than that of many modern-day animals.

Built for distance

Although too heavy to run fast, *Tyrannosaurus*'s long legs helped it cover long distances with ease.

SIMILAR TO MODERN ELEPHANTS, *TYRANNOSAURUS* COULD HEAR

Prime predator

Around 67–66 million years ago, the 6.5-ton *Tyrannosaurus* dominated North America. Incredibly agile, it could turn twice as fast compared to the lighter Cretaceous predators. Its large brain also allowed it to quickly process information about its surroundings. It was the perfect hunter.

Bone breaker

Tyrannosaurus was the strongest biting organism to ever live on land. Its long, banana-shaped teeth and formidable jaws could shatter the bones of its prey, then inflict enough damage to break up a carcass into bite-sized pieces.

Tyrannosaurus skull

Eagle eyes

Similar to a modern-day eagle, *Tyrannosaurus* had exceptional vision. This dinosaur could see a long way in front, giving it the advantage when attacking prey.

Bald eagle

Balancing act
The stiff tail helped this large dinosaur balance its very heavy head.

Lethal bite
Sharp teeth could crunch through the tough hide of its prey.

Sharp claws
These pointed claws were very strong and provided a steady foothold.

Daylight attack

Tyrannosaurus wasn't fast, but its forward-facing eyes and relatively large brain allowed it to execute an ambush perfectly. Here, the carnivorous predator attempts to bring down the herbivore *Triceratops* as it tries to flee.

Diminishing sea
The Western Interior Seaway had receded by the Late Cretaceous, leaving behind fossils of giant marine reptiles.

NORTH AMERICA

Warm and tropical
Triceratops enjoyed a warm and sometimes subtropical climate, with no annual cold spells.

Horns as weapons

Evidence shows that this dinosaur used its horns to attack other *Triceratops.* The discovery of healed gouges on the frills of some specimens were probably made by a similar individual. They were perhaps locking horns over mates, food, or territory.

Side view of an adult *Triceratops* skull

PACIFIC OCEAN

Flowery diet
As this dinosaur roamed the wooded plains, it fed mainly on flowering plants, also known as angiosperms.

Triceratops

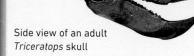

try-**SER**-a-tops

Roaming North America 68–66 million years ago, the 29.5-ft (9-m) long *Triceratops* was an intimidating creature, with its horned skull and dramatic frill. This tough herbivore could even take on the mighty *Tyrannosaurus.*

ATLANTIC OCEAN

PACIFIC OCEAN

INDIAN OCEAN

WHEN FIRST FOUND IN 1887, *TRICERATOPS* HORNS WERE

Pointed horns
he two brow horns could reach 4 ft (1.3 m) long, with sharp tips and strong bony cores.

Impressive frill
The neck frill was made of solid bone and covered in scaly skin. It was surrounded by bony spikes.

Changing with age

Many *Triceratops* fossils have been found, from full-grown adults to tiny juveniles. Using these finds, scientists have discovered that as they grew older, the horns changed shape, the frill became smoother, and the nose horn fused to the skull bones.

Sturdy stance
Triceratops supported its weight evenly on four legs.

Big beak
This dinosaur had a sharp, parrot-like beak.

THOUGHT TO BELONG TO AN EXTINCT BISON.

Spiky crowns
These may have been for show, but possibly also for defense.

Thick dome
Pachycephalosaurus fossils are quite rar and paleontologists usually only find the thick dome.

Combat specialist
The skull's dome was made up of a special type of bone that healed rapidly. *Pachycephalosaurus* fossils have been found with evidence of injuries, some of which were starting to heal. This suggests that they used their thick skulls to fight each other.

Bonehead
The skull's roof was made of a dome about 9.8 in (25 cm) thick. Adorned with spikes and knobs, the skull surrounded a long, slender brain. Research into its brain indicate this dinosaur had a decent sense of smell.

Pachycephalosaurus
PACK-ee-sef-ah-low-SORE-us

Weighing around half a ton and at 16.5 ft (5 m) in length, the thick, dome-headed *Pachycephalosaurus* is instantly recognizable. It lived 72–66 million years ago in the area we now know as North America, just before the extinction event that killed the dinosaurs.

Leaf eater
As *Pachycephalosaurus* roamed the region, it fed on leaves most of the time. However, it also may have eaten nuts and fruits.

ATLANTIC OCEAN

PACIFIC OCEAN

INDIAN OCEAN

Shrinking sea
The Western Interior Seaway had almost disappeared by now, allowing animals to move across the continent.

NORTH AMERICA

PACIFIC OCEAN

Rocky Mountains
This long, high range cut off many species of dinosaurs from the Pacific Ocean.

Mild climate
Pachycephalosaurus lived in a warm climate full of flowering plants, some of which it probably fed on.

Powerful legs
The animal's weight was supported by strong hind legs with four-toed feet.

Good balance
A stiff tail helped movement, allowing this herbivore to walk steadily on two legs.

COMPLETE *PACHYCEPHALOSAURUS* SKELETON.

Ross River, Yukon, Canada
Tracks from several types of dinosaurs have been found here, such as hadrosaurs, theropods, and rare ankylosaurs.

Prince Creek Formation, Alaska
The "dwarf" tyrannosaur *Nanuqsaurus* has been found here. Its smaller size was probably due to a shortage of food and cooler temperatures.

Earth today

NORTH AMERICA

Grande Cache, Alberta, Canada
10,000 footprints of large theropods and ankylosaurs are preserved on a cliff face.

KEY

● Dinosaur fossil site

Horseshoe Canyon Formation, Alberta, Canada

Dinosaur Park Formation, Alberta, Canada

Hell Creek Formation, Montana

Morrison Formation, Utah

Chinle Formation, New Mexico

Tyrannosaurus

In 1902, US paleontologist Barnum Brown discovered the dinosaur skeleton that scientist H. F. Osborn would first name *Tyrannosaurus* 3 years later.

ONE SECTION OF THE MORRISON FORMATION IS SO RICH IN JURASSIC

Fossil finds

Throughout the history of fossil hunting, North America has been one of the best places to find dinosaur bones. From northwestern Alaska and the remotest parts of Canada to fossil-rich rock formations in Mexico, this vast continent is a treasure trove for paleontologists.

Bay of Fundy, Nova Scotia, Canada
The 200 million-year-old rocks found here preserve evidence of a mass extinction that left dinosaurs dominating the land.

South Hadley, Massachusetts
In 1802, 12-year-old Pliny Moody discovered a slab of rock with strange marks. These were the first officially recognized dinosaur tracks. The three-toed prints were probably those of a theropod.

Dinosaur Valley State Park, Texas
The trackway along the Paluxy River, once an ancient ocean shoreline, preserved hundreds of footprints of giant sauropods and theropods.

Cerro del Pueblo Formation, Mexico
Various plant-eating dinosaurs have been found here, including ornithopods and ceratopsids.

Ornithomimus
This feathery theropod was named in the late 19th century during the "Bone Wars"—a bitter fossil hunting rivalry between Edward Cope and Othniel Marsh.

Major fossil sites

Horseshoe Canyon Formation, Alberta, Canada (Cretaceous)
Major find: *Albertosaurus*

Dinosaur Park Formation, Alberta, Canada (Cretaceous)
Major find: *Corythosaurus*

Hell Creek Formation, Montana (Cretaceous)
Major finds: *Tyrannosaurus, Ankylosaurus, Pachycephalosaurus*

Morrison Formation, Utah (Jurassic)
Major finds: *Stegosaurus, Diplodocus, Allosaurus, Ceratosaurus*

Chinle Formation, New Mexico (Triassic)
Major find: *Coelophysis*

Dinosaur bones in the rocks from the Morrison Formation in Utah.

SOUTH AMERICA

Horns and teeth
Few carnivores looked more formidable than *Carnotaurus*, with its bull-like horns and spiky teeth. This animal terrorized regions of South America around 70 million years ago.

Herrerasaurus

her-air-ah-**SORE**-us

One of the earliest dinosaurs to evolve, around 230 million years ago, *Herrerasaurus* stalked an area dominated by floodplains in the supercontinent of Gondwana. At 20 ft (6 m) long, it was a large, carnivorous predator.

230 MYA

Unusual jaw

A flexible joint in the lower jaw of *Herrerasaurus* allowed the bones to slide back and forth, helping it to grip struggling, live prey—similar to some modern lizards. Elasticlike ligaments created this flexibility, probably allowing the jaw to absorb shock during biting.

Fossilized
Herrerasaurus skull

Long hands
Three elongated, clawed fingers were useful for grasping prey. The outer two fingers were buried in the soft tissues of each hand.

Uncertain ancestry

Because of its great age and unusual anatomy, the position of *Herrerasaurus* in the dinosaur family tree is still uncertain. Recent research places it as closely related to sauropods, while older research generally suggests theropod ancestry.

THE SKULL BONES OF ONE INDIVIDUAL SHOW BITE MARKS THAT

Tall trees

Huge, 130-ft (40-m) tall, fossilized tree trunks have been found in the region, as well as ferns and horsetails.

Wet seasons

Strong, seasonal rainfall brought wet conditions to the region, which was otherwise dry.

G O N D W A N A

Argentinian fossils

Herrerasaurus fossils have been found in what is today the South American country of Argentina.

Active volcanoes

At this time, there was volcanic activity throughout the area. Volcanic ash covered the floodplains, providing plants with nutrients. The ash also preserved fossils for the future.

Shared habitat

Despite its formidable weaponry and large size, *Herrerasaurus* shared its habitat with even larger predators. Ancient reptiles such as *Saurosuchus* (above) were the very top predators of the region. Luckily for the dinosaurs, these had died out by the end of the Triassic.

Curved teeth

Backward-facing teeth helped *Herrerasaurus* prey on smaller reptiles, early dinosaurs, and mammal ancestors.

Stiff tail

Interlocking tail bones stabilized the tail.

APPEAR TO HAVE BEEN INFLICTED BY ANOTHER *HERRERASAURUS*.

Bird-beaked
A keratin beak covering the front of the jaws was perfect for biting off low-lying vegetation.

S O U T H
A M E R I C A

Strange skeleton

Chilesaurus possessed hind legs similar to those of a theropod. Its teeth were spatulate—flat and blunt, perfect for biting and chewing plant matter. Although this dinosaur looked like a carnivore in some ways, it certainly did not have the knifelike teeth of meat eaters such as the fearsome Cretaceous predator *Tyrannosaurus.*

Receding sea
Dropping sea levels exposed more land for *Chilesaurus* to inhabit.

Reconstruction of *Chilesaurus* skeleton

Volcanic activity
At this time, volcanic eruptions in the region may have killed or injured some *Chilesaurus,* as they weren't the quickest to escape.

Chilesaurus

chi-le-**SORE**-us

Balancing act
The long tail of the *Chilesaurus* helped to balance its body on its small legs.

A 10-ft (3-m) long herbivore, *Chilesaurus* roamed South America around 150 million years ago. Experts have struggled to find a place for it in the dinosaur family tree. Its body outline is similar to a carnivore, yet its birdlike hips look similar to an ornithischian dinosaur, such as *Stegosaurus.*

Air sacs
Neck bones had a hollow on each side filled with air sacs. These hollows make the bone lighter and are also found in modern birds.

Uncertain history
With birdlike hips similar to ornithischians and the body proportions of a theropod, placing *Chilesaurus* within the dinosaur family tree is tricky. While it has been interpreted as a member of each of the three major dinosaurian branches, it seems most likely that *Chilesaurus* was a theropod.

Poor runner
With an ankle and foot poorly adapted for running, *Chilesaurus* may have hidden from predators instead.

AFRICA

ATLANTIC OCEAN

PACIFIC OCEAN

INDIAN OCEAN

SOUTH AMERICA

Shifting land
At this time, Africa had fully separated from South America, and the Atlantic Ocean had started to form.

Big tooth
Giganotosaurus and its cousins are carcharodontosaurids, which means "shark-toothed lizards." Their thin, sawlike teeth—6 in (15 cm) long and made to slice through flesh—were set in a skull almost 6.5 ft (2 m) long.

Vanished rivers
Much of the rock where *Giganotosaurus* fossils were found revealed signs of complex river systems.

Hunting ground
Giganotosaurus is likely to have hunted among conifer forests and flowering plants.

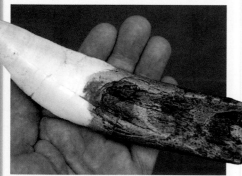

PACIFIC OCEAN

Rising Andes
Rapid sea floor spreading in the Atlantic and Pacific Oceans helped to push up the Andes Mountains in this region.

Giganotosaurus
GEEG-ah-NOTE-ih-SORE-us

In 1993, amateur fossil hunter Rubén Carolini alerted local scientists to an exposed leg bone he had found in the southernmost part of South America. Little did he know then that the bone belonged to one of the largest carnivores ever to walk the Earth—and one that ruled at the very top of the food chain.

Giant killers

About 100 million years ago, a group of allosaurs began to grow to huge sizes, perhaps because they had few competitors and plenty of large prey. These hunters included the 40-ft (12-m) long *Giganotosaurus*.

Steady temperature
The body temperature of *Giganotosaurus* remained steady compared to many other dinosaurs. Some experts think this is why it grew so rapidly.

Three claws
This dinosaur's arm bones have not yet been found, but it probably had three fingers like other allosaurs.

Walking pace
It was once thought that *Giganotosaurus* could run quickly, but modern research suggests that it probably kept to a fast walk.

Quick bite
Giganotosaurus did not have especially powerful jaws but could make rapid bites, one after another.

TO 125 ADULT PEOPLE OF AVERAGE SIZE.

Fighting it out

There are advantages to being a giant. Even though the smaller *Ekrixinatosaurus* was the first to find the carcass, *Giganotosaurus* has muscled its way in to take over the spoils. If it survives, *Ekrixinatosaurus* will have to wait for any scraps left behind.

Continents apart
At the time, South America and North America were not connected as they are today.

Holding up
The largest of the bones that made up the spine and tail, called vertebrae, was 5 ft (1.6 m) high and helped prevent the body from sagging.

SOUTH AMERICA

Argentinian fossils
Argentinosaurus gets its name from the country where its fossils were first discovered—modern-day Argentina.

Dry climate
Evidence from fossil sites suggests that *Argentinosaurus* probably lived in an arid environment.

Long reach
The long neck may have helped *Argentinosaurus* to browse efficiently without using up too much energy moving around.

Dinosaur nursery
In 1997, in the southern tip of South America, a large sauropod nesting ground was found. The dinosaurs had dug the ground and laid 15–34 eggs. This revealed that dinosaurs such as *Argentinosaurus* nested together.

Sauropod egg fragments

Digestion
Plant matter was probably broken down by bacteria in the gut to release its energy.

BULKY *ARGENTINOSAURUS* COULD ONLY AMBLE ALONG AT A SLOW

Supporting skeleton

One of the heaviest land animals ever to exist, *Argentinosaurus* needed strongly built legs. This formed a natural supportive arch for its body, putting the least possible stress on the joints.

South American giant

Argentinosaurus is known only from an incomplete skeleton found in Argentina. Based on this, scientists have worked out that it would have weighed around 88 tons—or about the same as six fire engines.

Heavy muscles

Bulky triceps muscles at the back of the forelimbs helped support the dinosaur's weight as it roamed around.

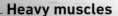

Argentinosaurus

ARE-jen-teen-oh-SORE-us

One of the colossal sauropods known as titanosaurs, *Argentinosaurus* was supersized even among its cousins. Reaching 115 ft (35 m) in length, this herbivore roamed South America 90 million years ago. This giant ate a lot, probably 235–500 lb (106–230 kg) of food every day—that's as heavy as 30–65 bricks!

Carnotaurus

car-noe-**TOR**-us

Horned beast
Two 6-in (15-cm) long,
cone-shaped horns
protruded above
each eye socket.

A 26-ft (8-m) long predator, *Carnotaurus* was a threatening presence in Late Cretaceous South America, around 70 million years ago. Named after the ancient Greek for "meat-eating bull," this fast-running dinosaur was armed with a horned skull, sharp teeth, and a desire to kill and eat anything, big or small.

Shoving matches

After finding and studying a well-preserved *Carnotaurus* skull from Argentina, some paleontologists suggested that the dinosaur's horns were used to shove one another, perhaps to compete for mates.

Carnotaurus skull

Carnivorous bull

The theories about the feeding habits of *Carnotaurus* are somewhat controversial. Some scientists believe it was a killer of big game, taking down large sauropods. Others argue that its narrow skull and jaw shape resulted in a weak bite, better suited for small prey, such as ornithopods.

FOSSILIZED SKIN IMPRESSIONS HAVE SHOWN LARGE, BUMPY

Slender jaw
Although the lower jaw was very slim, it could snap shut quickly—ideal for grabbing small prey.

Tiny arms
Its arms were tiny, lacked a movable elbow, and had no role in hunting.

Strong muscles
Almost 309 lb (140 kg) of muscle attached to the back of each leg helped this predator to run very fast.

Big tail
A long, rigid tail provided balance for *Carnotaurus* but hindered its agility.

Plant life
Diverse flora in the region may have led to a large number of herbivores for *Carnotaurus* to prey upon.

SOUTH AMERICA

Seasonal prey
Distinct wet and dry seasons probably changed the amount of prey available to *Carnotaurus* throughout the year.

High seas
At this time, the warm climate prevented the formation of icecaps, leading to an increase in global sea levels. As a result, some of South America as we know it today was under water.

Speedster
Carnotaurus was perhaps one of the fastest of the large theropods. The modified bones in this dinosaur's tail could support large tail muscles, helping it to reach speeds up to 30 mph (50 km/h)—roughly the same as the speed of a lion. While useful for hunting, these sizable muscles may have cost *Carnotaurus* the ability to turn quickly.

ATLANTIC OCEAN

PACIFIC OCEAN

INDIAN OCEAN

Eoraptor

One of the earliest dinosaurs known, this 3-ft (1-m) long animal was found in the rocky landscape of the Ischigualasto Formation in Argentina. *Eoraptor* probably hunted small reptiles.

Itapecuru Group, Brazil
Dinosaur remains from sauropods and theropods have been found at this site in Maranhão state.

Girón Formation, Colombia
One of the rare Jurassic sauropods to be found outside Argentina was excavated here.

Earth today

S O U T H   A M E R I C A

Vilquechico Group, Peru
Dinosaur tracks have been found at this site just to the north of Lake Titicaca.

Fossil finds

South America

Fossils of some of the earliest and largest dinosaurs ever have been unearthed in South America. However, with the dense Amazon rainforest, South America can be a challenging place to search for fossils. The southern parts of the continent yield the most finds.

KEY

🔴 **Dinosaur fossil site**

Valley of the Dinosaurs, Paraíba, Brazil
Various dinosaur tracks from theropods and ornithopods have been found in the Rio de Peixe Basin.

Bauru Group, Brazil
Sauropod and theropod remains from the Late Cretaceous have been found at this site in the Mato Grosso region.

Minas Gerais, Brazil
Theropod and sauropod remains from the Late Cretaceous have been found in the geological formations of this state.

Major fossil sites

Ischigualasto Formation, San Juan Province, Argentina (Triassic)
Major finds: *Eoraptor, Herrerasaurus*

Huincul Formation, Neuquén Province, Argentina (Cretaceous)
Major find: *Argentinosaurus*

Candeleros Formation, Neuquén Province, Argentina (Cretaceous)
Major find: *Giganotosaurus*

La Colonia Formation, Chubut Province, Argentina (Cretaceous)
Major find: *Carnotaurus*

Toqui Formation, Ayén Region, Chile (Jurassic)
Major find: *Chilesaurus*

Ischigualasto Formation is also called "Valley of the Moon."

Santa Maria Formation, Brazil
This Late Triassic ecosystem was unearthed in southern Brazil. Fossils include the small predatory dinosaur *Staurikosaurus*.

Entre Rios, Argentina
Titanosaur bones and teeth from ankylosaurs and theropods have been found here.

Candeleros Formation, Neuquén Province, Argentina

Cerro Fortaleza Formation, Argentina
The giant titanosaur *Puertasaurus*, the theropod *Orkoraptor*, and the ornithopod *Talenkauen* have been recovered here in southern Patagonia.

Ischigualasto Formation, San Juan Province, Argentina

Huincul Formation, Neuquén Province, Argentina

La Colonia Formation, Chubut Province, Argentina

Toqui Formation, Ayén Region, Chile

EUROPE

Ancient bird
Crow-sized and the oldest-known bird, *Archaeopteryx* had a bony tail, clawed wings, and toothed jaws. Living in the dry, sparse landscape of Late Jurassic Europe, it could fly only short distances.

Leafy teeth

This early relative of sauropods sliced and chopped plant material with its leaf-shaped teeth.

PANGEA

Efficient lungs

This dinosaur most likely had birdlike lungs, which supplied a lot of oxygen quickly, fueling fast growth and movement.

Powerful arms

The arms were strong with large claws, perhaps used to grasp food or for fighting.

ATLANTIC
OCEAN

PACIFIC
OCEAN

INDIAN
OCEAN

Growing fast

An adult *Plateosaurus* could reach lengths of 16–33 ft (5–10 m). Studies of the bones also show that this dinosaur could grow very fast— a trait that helped its later cousins to become truly gigantic.

Two legs or four?

Scientists have long debated how *Plateosaurus* moved. In the past, some experts argued that it walked on four legs like a lizard, while others thought it hopped like a kangaroo. However, modern research suggests that the arms would have been of little use for moving on all fours, and that the animal's limbs were perfectly built for a two-legged gait.

Plateosaurus skeletal reconstruction

Need for speed

Long toes and legs gave *Plateosaurus* the power to walk at a fast pace, but not run.

PLATEOSAURUS POSSESSED SERRATED, CONE-SHAPED TEETH AT

Flexible neck
This dinosaur's long, bendy neck allowed it to reach for nutritious leaves in tall trees.

Mud traps
After torrential downpours, pools of sticky mud were sometimes left behind. These could be death traps for a heavy adult *Plateosaurus*. Such sites became boneyards for future scientists to discover.

Green diet
Vegetation in the Northern Hemisphere consisted largely of conifer trees and ferns, which provided suitable food for *Plateosaurus*.

TETHYS OCEAN

Long, strong tail
Flexible and packed with muscle, the tail helped to balance the body and propel the legs.

Plateosaurus

PLATE-ee-oh-SORE-us

Around 210 million years ago, *Plateosaurus* was a common dinosaur in the supercontinent of Pangea. With so many well-preserved skeletons discovered in what is now Europe, experts have learned a great deal about this fascinating herbivore, including its diet and anatomy.

THE FRONT OF ITS JAW, WITH LEAF-SHAPED TEETH AT THE BACK.

Muddy swamps

Pterosaurs swoop by two *Plateosaurus* making their way through a swamp, while a prehistoric turtle stays at a safe distance. Millions of years later, the tracks left behind by these dinosaurs will be preserved, as the mud solidifies into fossil footprints.

Ophthalmosaurus fossil found in Peterborough, UK

Giant eye

The eyes of *Ophthalmosaurus* were as much as 8.7 in (22 cm) wide and were among the largest eyes of any animal that's ever lived. These would have allowed it to see in deep, dark waters, up to 1,640 ft (500 m) below the surface.

Vertical fin

The ichthyosaur tail fin was vertical, like that of a shark or tuna. *Ophthalmosaurus* swam by beating this powerful tail from side to side.

Streamlined body

Ophthalmosaurus had a torpedo-shaped body, smooth skin, and paddlelike limbs. The tail was powerful and looked like that of a shark. It also shared its body shape with some of today's sea creatures, such as sailfish.

Deep vision

As a predator, this marine reptile would have relied on its excellent eyesight to chase fish and squid, often at great depth.

Powerful paddles

Thick, powerful forepaddles were used in steering.

Ophthalmosaurus

off-**THAL**-mo-**SORE**-us

This Jurassic animal is not a dinosaur, but belongs to a group called ichthyosaurs. Descended from lizardlike land animals, *Ophthalmosaurus* was 20 ft (6 m) long and swam in seas worldwide 150 million years ago.

Hispanic Corridor
A seaway between modern-day Europe and South America, called the Hispanic Corridor, meant the coasts of both regions were home to very similar animals.

L A U R A S I A

European seas
Shallow seas covered much of what is Europe today at this time, and clays and muds were being laid down to form thick layers of rock.

ATLANTIC OCEAN

PACIFIC OCEAN

INDIAN OCEAN

New continents
Laurasia and Gondwana were splitting apart and were almost fully separate at this time. Each continent was also breaking up into smaller sections.

G O N D W A N A

Catching prey
Long, slender jaws and conical, pointed teeth were ideal for grabbing slippery, fast-moving prey.

Staying stable
A triangular dorsal fin helped *Ophthalmosaurus* remain stable while swimming at speed.

Warm climate
Global conditions were warm and even the seas in the far south of the globe were not cold.

OPHTHALMOSAURUS, WHICH IN GREEK MEANS "EYE-LIZARD."

150 MYA
ATLANTIC OCEAN
PACIFIC OCEAN
INDIAN OCEAN

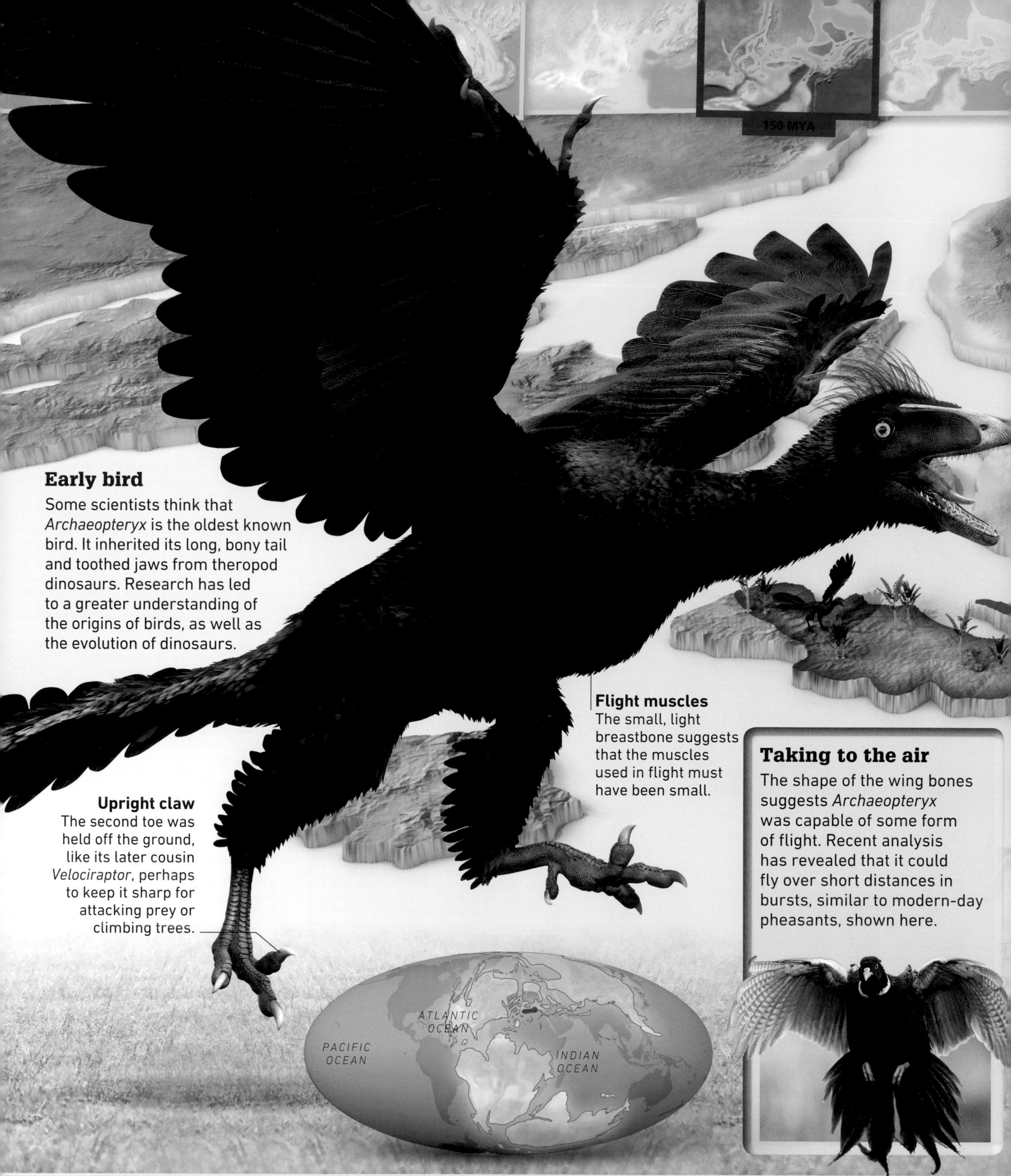

Early bird

Some scientists think that *Archaeopteryx* is the oldest known bird. It inherited its long, bony tail and toothed jaws from theropod dinosaurs. Research has led to a greater understanding of the origins of birds, as well as the evolution of dinosaurs.

Flight muscles
The small, light breastbone suggests that the muscles used in flight must have been small.

Upright claw
The second toe was held off the ground, like its later cousin *Velociraptor*, perhaps to keep it sharp for attacking prey or climbing trees.

Taking to the air

The shape of the wing bones suggests *Archaeopteryx* was capable of some form of flight. Recent analysis has revealed that it could fly over short distances in bursts, similar to modern-day pheasants, shown here.

ANALYSIS OF A SET OF BONES IN THE EYE, CALLED THE SCLERAL

Toothed bird
Lining the jaws were 50 small teeth, which were perfect for an animal-based diet.

Clawed wings
Archaeopteryx retained the clawed hands of theropod dinosaurs, though they were unlikely to have been used to capture prey.

Bony tail
A long, bony tail, complete with feathers, provided some balance when walking on the ground.

LAURASIA

Salty lagoons
Extremely salty, oxygen-poor water helped to preserve the delicate features of *Archaeopteryx* for millions of years by preventing decomposition.

European archipelago
Surrounded by warm, shallow seas, Europe at this time was split up into small islands. A vast portion of this is what we call Germany today.

Aerial dominance
Although *Archaeopteryx* could fly, skies throughout the region at this time were dominated by several types of pterosaurs.

Archaeopteryx

ar-kee-**OP**-ter-ix

First discovered in Germany in 1861, the exquisitely preserved fossils of *Archaeopteryx* revealed a crow-sized animal that could fly, although not very well. It inhabited the wooded islands of Late Jurassic Europe, 151–146 million years ago.

Fossilized feather
Studies of this fossilized *Archaeopteryx* feather have shown that it was black and had a structure just like that of modern bird feathers. This would have helped the animal to fly short distances.

RING, SUGGESTS *ARCHAEOPTERYX* WAS ACTIVE DURING THE DAY.

N O R T H
A M E R I C A

E U R O P E

Dangerous habitat
The Mediterranean-like climate in this area came with hazards such as forest fires and flooding.

European islands
During the Early Cretaceous, much of Europe was made up of islands separated by shallow seas. This region is modern-day Spain.

ATLANTIC
OCEAN

PACIFIC
OCEAN

INDIAN
OCEAN

Spiky specimen

When first found, a spiky bone was thought to come from the nose of *Iguanodon*. Experts now know it was attached to the forelimbs. Some scientists think it was for defense; others argue it was for foraging.

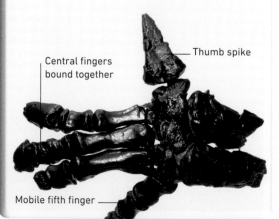

Central fingers bound together

Thumb spike

Mobile fifth finger

Muscular thighs
Iguanodon could rear up and run on its hind legs—useful for both intimidation and escaping danger.

Long arms
These allowed *Iguanodon* to move around on four limbs.

FOSSILIZED BRAIN TISSUE FOUND IN AN *IGUANODON* SPECIMEN

Plant diet
Horsetails, ferns, and low-lying conifer branches may have all nourished the bulky *Iguanodon*.

Scaly skin
Iguanodon was covered with tough skin that protected it from infections and scratches.

Plant predator
A sharp beak and iguanalike teeth, from which *Iguanodon* gets its name, helped to grind up plant food.

Important find
In 1822, the Englishman Gideon Mantell or his wife Mary found fossilized teeth. At first, scientists believed these teeth belonged to a big lizard, but later realized that they were from a gigantic reptile very different from modern lizards. In 1878, complete *Iguanodon* skeletons were found in Belgium.

Iguanodon
ig-**WAH**-no-don

In 1825, *Iguanodon* became famous as one of the first dinosaurs to be formally named. This plant-eating, heavyweight ornithopod roamed areas of Europe 140–110 million years ago. Studies of its thick bones suggest that adults could reach lengths of 33 ft (10 m) and weigh up to 4.5 tons.

Fused wrist
The bones of the wrist were fused together, helping *Iguanodon* bear weight on its front limbs.

FROM THE UK RESEMBLES LIVING CROCODILIANS AND BIRDS.

British icon
The first *Baryonyx* fossil was found in Surrey, in the south of England.

Wetland habitat
The many rivers and lakes found in Europe during the Early Cretaceous provided a home for *Baryonyx*, allowing it to coexist with other large predators.

Iberian hunter
Fossils have been found as far as Spain.

ATLANTIC OCEAN

PACIFIC OCEAN

INDIAN OCEAN

Baryonyx

bah-ree-**ON**-ix

The 26-ft (8-m) long *Baryonyx* evolved to exploit a different habitat to other theropods: water. Its long skull and conical teeth were perfect for catching slippery fish at the edges of rivers and lakes across a wide area of Europe 125 million years ago.

Bipedal locomotion
Typical of two-legged theropods, *Baryonyx* balanced its body over its hind legs.

ALTHOUGH MOST BARYONYX BONES ARE UNEARTHED IN EUROPE,

Toothy grin
Sixty-four small teeth lined the lower jaw—more than the average theropod.

EUROPE

Hunting strategies
The details of the predatory lifestyle of *Baryonyx* are still debated. However, most experts describe this dinosaur as a "generalist" predator, exploiting prey in both water and land, including thick-scaled fish and juvenile dinosaurs.

Muscular tail
Like many other theropods, the long, powerful tail provided the balance needed to walk and run.

Stomach contents
The scales of the fish *Lepidotes* were found in the stomach of the original *Baryonyx* specimen. This led to the view that this dinosaur and its cousins ate a variety of organisms and differed from other theropods in including fish in their diet.

Heavy claw
The function of the 10-in (25-cm) claw is unclear. It is most commonly thought to be a tool for hooking fish out of water, much like a grizzly bear does today.

Robust arms
Paleontologists still question how the heavily built arms were used. They may have been used to catch fish or open their carcasses.

Fossil of *Baryonyx* thumb claw

SOME NORTH AFRICAN FOSSILS MAY ALSO BELONG TO THIS DINOSAUR.

79

ATLANTIC
OCEAN

PACIFIC
OCEAN

INDIAN
OCEAN

Low-lying plants
This herbivore probably ate ferns and horsetails, as its low body was unable to reach taller plants.

Warm climate
Polacanthus habitats, including what we call Spain today, were characterized by warm summers and mild winters.

ALPINE OCEAN

Polacanthus
pol-a-**CAN**-thus

Strong tongue
Polacanthus had powerful tongue muscles, enabling them to tear up tough plant material.

At 16 ft (5 m) long, *Polacanthus* was not the largest herbivore to march its way through parts of Early Cretaceous Europe, around 125 million years ago, but it did have some of the best armor. A shield of bone covered its hips, while large spikes protected its neck and back.

POLACANTHUS MEANS "MANY THORNS" IN ANCIENT GREEK, IN

Shallow seas
Waterways separated western Europe from the rest of the Eurasian continent.

Long guts
The broad hips suggest it had long intestines to digest plant material.

Hip shield
A single, fused sheet of bone covered the upper surface of the hip region to protect the hip bones and thigh muscles.

Unarmed
Polacanthus and its closest cousins lacked a tail club, but small spikes along the tail may have been enough to deter predators.

Blood supply
The plates and spikes have shown imprints of blood vessels, which may have supplied growing tissue with blood.

Rare creature
Not much is known of *Polacanthus* because fossils are rare. While some bones from parts of continental Europe have been assigned to this dinosaur, it is mainly known from fossils found in the UK. From these, there is enough material to reconstruct this animal as a wide, armored herbivore.

Armored beast
Bones called osteoderms grew directly from the skin of *Polacanthus* and many of its cousins. Smaller bones known as ossicles grew around them, sometimes forming plates of armor that protected them from predators.

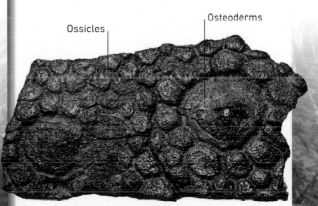

Ossicles

Osteoderms

Small part of fossilized *Polacanthus* skin

ATLANTIC OCEAN

PACIFIC OCEAN

INDIAN OCEAN

Inland lakes
A complex system of lakes and swamps served as a habitat for *Pelecanimimus*.

Excellent preservation
Microorganisms in lakes ma have covered *Pelecanimimus* remains, preserving them as fossils.

Different teeth
Pelecanimimus specimens show a condition known as heterodonty—the possession of different-shaped teeth. The front teeth were broad, while those at the back were bladelike. Both types lacked serrated edges.

Reconstructed *Pelecanimimus* skull

High biodiversity
More than 200 species of plant and animal life lived in and around the swamps of Early Cretaceous Spain.

Fleshy crest
This may have been used to attract mates, similar to the soft tissues on the heads of some birds today.

Pelecanimimus
PEL-lee-can-ah-ME-mus

This dinosaur's jaws were lined with many teeth, making *Pelecanimimus* different from other later, usually toothless, ostrichlike dinosaurs called ornithomimosaurs. These teeth may have helped this lightweight, 8-ft (2.5-m) long theropod to slice up food in Europe around 125 million years ago.

Avian ankle
A hingelike ankle is a trait that unites all dinosaurs and modern birds.

Rare teeth
Only a few ornithomimosaurs possessed teeth like *Pelecanimimus*—for example, the Mongolian *Harpymimus*. Later species lost them in favor of beaks.

Fuzzy theropod
Pelecanimimus was found with basic feathers covering its body. However, some experts believe these are possibly muscle fibers.

ALPINE OCEAN

Perfect preservation

The Las Hoyas site in Spain, where *Pelecanimimus* was discovered, is famous for its exquisitely preserved fossils. This includes some soft tissues of the dinosaur's throat and the crest on its head.

Feathered display
Arm feathers have not been found, but were possibly present and may have had a role in display to attract mates.

Pelican mimic

The preservation of stretchy skin under the jaw, called a gular pouch, led some scientists to argue *Pelecanimimus* stored its food in its throat, much like a modern-day pelican. Although the diet of this dinosaur is unknown, some experts suggest it caught fish.

Speedy runner
Elongated foot bones and long legs indicate this small dinosaur was speedy—good for both hunting and escaping predators.

Giant of the skies

Although its bones were thick and heavy, this pterosaur was light for its size and could definitely fly. *Hatzegopteryx* could walk and run on the ground, too.

Huge wings

Wing membranes stretched from the tips of the fourth fingers to the body and leg.

Skull crest

A bony crest probably ran along the top of the skull and upper jaw.

ATLANTIC OCEAN

PACIFIC OCEAN

INDIAN OCEAN

Wing supports

The wing was mostly supported by long hand bones and an elongated, thick fourth finger that extended to the tip of the wing.

Hatzegopteryx

HAT-zeg-OP-ter-ix

Of all the flying reptiles known as pterosaurs, *Hatzegopteryx* was the biggest. Taking to the skies around 70 million years ago, it had a wingspan of around 33 ft (10 m) and stood 10 ft (3 m) tall at the shoulder. With its thick neck and storklike jaws, it could catch prey the size of a human.

Toothless

The group of pterosaurs to which *Hatzegopteryx* belonged did not have teeth.

HATZEGOPTERYX HAD A SKULL MEASURING AROUND 10 FT (3 M)

Hateg Island
This ancient Cretaceous landmass, known as Hateg Island, is part of Romania today. It is the location of the only known *Halzegopteryx* fossils.

TETHYS OCEAN

SOUTHERN EUROPE

Forests
Hatzegopteryx roamed a forested region that was dotted with tropical plants.

Powerful bite
The powerful beak and jaws were made of thick bone.

Wingspan
Hatzegopteryx had a wingspan about equal to that of a small plane. Large ridges on its wing bones, which mark the points where muscles attached, show that the muscles were huge and powerful.

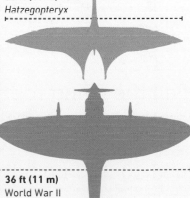

33 ft (10 m)
Hatzegopteryx

36 ft (11 m)
World War II
Spitfire

Folded wings
The wings could be folded away when the animal walked on the ground.

Fingers for walking
Three short, clawed fingers were used in walking.

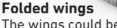

Today's catch

Hatzegopteryx was not a dinosaur but a flying reptile, or pterosaur. It was one of the largest pterosaurs ever, with a wingspan of 33 ft (10 m) and a skull around 6.5 ft (2 m) long. Its powerful neck and strong jaws allowed it to grab and swallow prey such as this turkey-sized dinosaur.

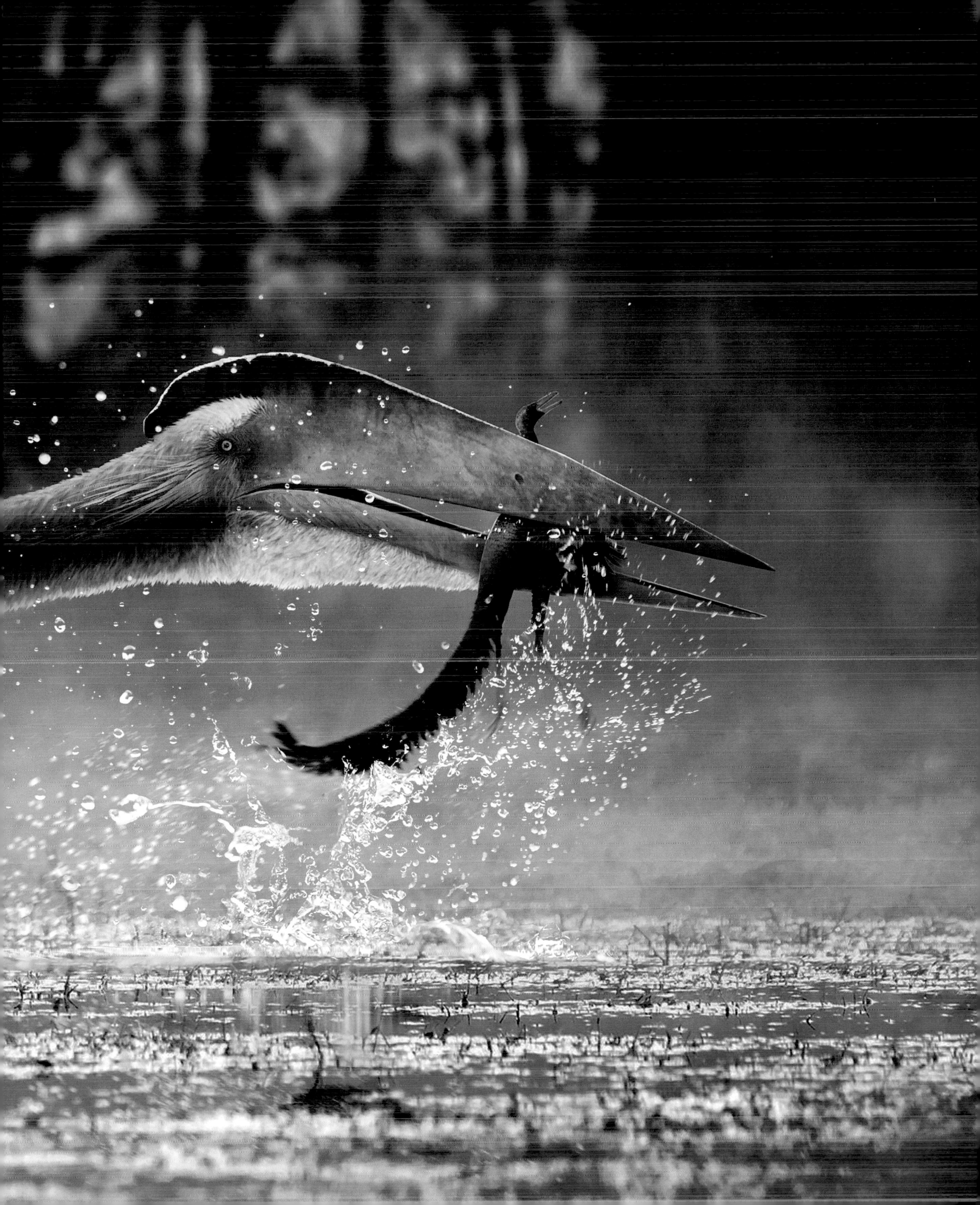

Earth today

Lunde Formation, North Sea
Upper Triassic rocks here preserve the footprints of early dinosaurs, including midsized predators with birdlike feet.

Valtos Sandstone Formation, Scotland
Dinosaur bones found in the Middle Jurassic rocks of the island of Skye reveal the presence of sauropods and theropods.

Oxford Clay Formation, UK

Solnhofen Formation, Germany

Bernissart, Belgium

Wessex Formation, UK

Archaeopteryx
The famous "first bird" comes from the limestone quarries of Bavaria, Germany. There are currently only 12 known *Archaeopteryx* specimens.

Fossil finds

Europe

Europe is where our knowledge of dinosaurs and other prehistoric animals began. Dinosaurs were discovered here before they were recognized elsewhere in the world. Rich fossil sites in the UK, Portugal, Germany, Hungary, Romania, and other countries continue to yield new species to this day.

Castellan Formation, La Rioja, Spain
Sauropods, theropods, stegosaurs, and others have been found in these Lower Cretaceous rocks.

Lourinhã Formation, Portugal

A FOSSIL FOUND IN ENGLAND IN 1676 WAS PROBABLY A *MEGALOSAURUS*

Major fossil sites

Bernissart, Belgium (Cretaceous)
Major find: *Iguanodon*

Oxford Clay Formation, UK (Jurassic)
Major finds: *Loricatosaurus,
Callovosaurus, Eustreptospondylus*

Wessex Formation, UK (Cretaceous)
Major finds: *Polacanthus,
Hypsilophodon, Iguanodon, Neovenator*

Lourinhã Formation, Portugal
(Jurassic)
Major finds: *Allosaurus, Ceratosaurus*

Solnhofen Formation, Germany
(Jurassic)
Major finds: *Compsognathus, Juravenator,
Ostromia, Archaeopteryx*

Pietraroia
Plattenkalk,
Italy (Cretaceous)
Major find:
Scipionyx

Fossil-bearing limestone
occurs at many places
across Europe, such as
Bavaria, in Germany.

**Moskvoretskaya
Formation, Russia**
The Middle Jurassic rocks here
have yielded prehistoric
reptiles, amphibians,
mammals, and theropod teeth.

EUROPE

Rybushka Formation, Russia
The Upper Cretaceous rocks have
yielded bones from animals of
the sea or nearby coasts, including
pterosaurs, plesiosaurs, and seabirds.

**Pietraroia
Plattenkalk,
Italy**

KEY

● **Dinosaur
fossil site**

LEG BONE, BUT AT THAT TIME, LOCALS THOUGHT IT WAS A GIANT HUMAN!

89

AFRICA

Aquatic predators
Three slender *Mesosaurus* swirl above a Pangean lake bed, their needlelike teeth ready to snatch prey. These swimming reptiles lived in cool, fresh waters around 290 million years ago.

WESTERN PANGEA

ATLANTIC OCEAN

PACIFIC OCEAN

INDIAN OCEAN

Cool lagoons

Mesosaurus lived in cool, salty lagoons or lakes across western Pangea.

Plant life

At this time, the land in the area nearby was covered in forest, mostly formed of the tree-sized plant *Glossopteris*.

Ice Age

Mesosaurus lived in the Permian world before dinosaurs existed and when parts of Earth were in the grip of an Ice Age.

Mesosaurus skull

Lake-dwelling lizard

Mesosaurus was one of the earliest aquatic reptiles, inhabiting the ancient supercontinent Pangea around 290 million years ago. It lived a semiaquatic lifestyle, spending much of its time searching for food in cool lakes.

Needle teeth

Mesosaurus was equipped with long jaws lined with many thin, needlelike teeth. Too delicate to handle large prey, these teeth were most likely used to grab small, swimming crustaceans, the ancestors of today's shrimp and crabs.

Buoyant bones

Dense ribs may have helped with buoyancy.

THE DISCOVERY OF *MESOSAURUS* FOSSILS ON TWO SEPARATE

Mesosaurus

mee-so-**SORE**-us

At 3 ft (1 m) long, *Mesosaurus* was not a dinosaur but an ancient swimming reptile that lived in lakes. Fossil finds in southern Africa and South America show that these two areas were joined when this creature was alive.

Built-in paddle
The long, deep tail could be used like a paddle when swimming.

High nostrils
The nostrils sat high up, close to the eyes.

Webbed feet
Mesosaurus had webbed fingers and toes to help it swim.

EASTERN PANGEA

Lystrosaurus
LIS-trow-SORE-us

This pudgy herbivore lived in Pangea 250 million years ago, during the Late Permian and Early Triassic. Several species are known, most of which were 3–6 ft (1–2 m) long. *Lystrosaurus* is not a dinosaur but belonged to a group called the dicynodont therapsids, a group closely related to mammals.

Hardy survivor

Lystrosaurus was tough and could survive in harsh, dry places. Although fossils have only been found in the northern and southern parts of Pangea, it probably lived throughout this region.

Sprawling gait

Unlike most modern mammals, the limbs of *Lystrosaurus* stuck out sideways from its body, like those of a reptile.

Burrow dweller

Fossils show that *Lystrosaurus* took shelter in burrows, probably to escape the heat of the day and cold of the night. It may have used its hands and beak when digging.

Broad body

Like all dicynodonts, *Lystrosaurus* had a broad, barrel-shaped body. Its large guts helped it digest tough plant food.

THIS THERAPSID'S TWO TUSKLIKE CANINE TEETH

PANGEA

ATLANTIC
OCEAN

PACIFIC
OCEAN

INDIAN
OCEAN

Island dweller
Islands and peninsulas to the northeast of Pangea now form parts of China, where *Lystrosaurus* fossils have been discovered.

Two teeth
The word dicynodont means "two canine teeth." Most dicynodonts were toothless apart from their two tusklike upper canines.

Lystrosaurus skull

Blunt beak
The mouth was covered with a tough hornlike beak, which helped *Lystrosaurus* bite through tough leaves and stems.

PANTHALASSIC OCEAN

Wide range
Lystrosaurus ranged across modern-day India, South Africa, and Antarctica.

WERE PROBABLY USED FOR DEFENSE OR DISPLAY.

Giraffatitan

ji-**RAF**-a-**TIE**-tan

An African giant, *Giraffatitan* towered over most other Late Jurassic dinosaurs. This 66-ft (20-m) long herbivore held its head 39 ft (12 m) above the ground, allowing it to access vegetation almost no other plant eater could reach.

SOUTH AMERICA

Andes forming
The formation of the Andes Mountains was underway at this time, with oceanic plates moving under South America.

Long neck
The number of bones in the neck of *Giraffatitan* is still unknown, but has been estimated at around 13—almost twice as many as a giraffe. Some researchers believe small muscles in the neck helped to pump blood to the head.

Giraffatitan neck bone fossil

Long-limbed
Giraffatitan's arms were longer than its legs, providing extra height when feeding.

TO FUEL ITS BODY,

Shearing bite
Wear on the teeth suggests it stripped leaves off branches rather than cutting them.

Tendaguru ecosystem
Found in the Tendaguru beds of Tanzania, *Giraffatitan* lived in conifer-rich inland habitats 154–142 million years ago. Nearer the coast, saltwater lagoons could be found, but offered little in terms of food for these giants.

Major discovery
An expedition to Tendaguru between 1909 and 1913 uncovered 248 tons of dinosaur bones, including those of *Giraffatitan*.

AFRICA

Absent Atlantic Ocean
At this time, South America and Africa were still joined. However, they were starting to move apart, gradually breaking up this ancient landmass.

Heavyweight herbivore
Recent estimates for the mass of *Giraffatitan* suggest it weighed around 33 tons—the equivalent of around five modern-day African elephants.

Air sacs
A complex system of air sacs in the vertebrae lightened the neck.

TETHYS OCEAN

PACIFIC OCEAN

ATLANTIC OCEAN

INDIAN OCEAN

Supporting tail
The tail's muscles attached to its thighs enabled it to walk quickly.

GIRAFFATITAN ATE UP TO 243 LB (110 KG) OF PLANT MATTER EACH DAY.

97

Near the water

This dinosaur probably did not roam far from the water-loving forests in its range.

Spinosaurus skull

Sail back

Large extensions of the back vertebrae formed a distinctive sail, which was perhaps used as a showy display feature.

Aquatic hunter

The narrow jaw, conical teeth, and rearward position of the nostrils suggest that *Spinosaurus* was an expert fish catcher. Chemical analysis of the teeth shows that they generally match those of modern semiaquatic reptiles such as crocodiles.

THE LONGEST OF THE BONY SPINES THAT MADE UP THE "SAIL"

Spinosaurus
SPINE-oh-SORE-us

The largest known theropod at 50 ft (15 m) long, *Spinosaurus* patrolled the floodplains of North Africa 90–75 million years ago. The first specimen found was lost during World War II, so this predator long remained shrouded in mystery. Recent finds have allowed paleontologists to reconstruct this remarkable creature.

Fossil finds
Spinosaurus mainly ate fish. Most of the other fossils found in modern-day North Africa have been carnivores. Very few plant-eating dinosaurs have been unearthed in this area.

PACIFIC OCEAN

ATLANTIC OCEAN

INDIAN OCEAN

Good swimmer?
Early analysis suggested that *Spinosaurus* spent most of its time in water. However, recent research argues that it was not a good swimmer. Computer models developed by experts indicate that it could not dive and swam no better than any other theropod. The debate continues.

Nasal crest
A small, fanlike crest on the snout might have been used for display.

Mobile neck
This dinosaur's flexible neck allowed it to strike fast, both on land and in water.

Long jaw
The skull was around 6 ft (2 m) long, with large teeth at the front to help skewer slippery prey.

Short legs
This animal may have had relatively short legs.

A fish dinner

An unlucky lungfish has been snared by a sail-backed *Spinosaurus* prowling the riverbanks for prey. This dinosaur will take its catch to a more secluded area, a safe distance from the watchful eyes of the crocodilelike *Elosuchus*.

Tataouine Basin, Tunisia
This region is known for the remains of giant crocodilian relatives, as well as hundreds of theropod teeth.

Bahariya Formation, Egypt

Earth today

Iouaridène Formation, Morocco
More than 1,500 dinosaur footprints have been found in the Late Jurassic rocks of the High Atlas Mountains.

A F R I C A

Elrhaz Formation, Niger

Tiourarén Formation, Niger

Major fossil sites

Bahariya Formation, Egypt (Cretaceous).
Major finds: *Paralititan, Aegyptosaurus, Spinosaurus, Carcharodontosaurus*

Tiourarén Formation, Niger (Jurassic).
Major finds: *Jobaria, Afrovenator*

Elrhaz Formation, Niger (Cretaceous).
Major finds: *Suchomimus, Nigersaurus, Ouranosaurus*

Bushveld Sandstone Formation, South Africa (Triassic).
Major find: *Massospondylus*

Upper Kirkwood Formation, South Africa (Cretaceous).
Major finds: *Nqwebasaurus, Paranthodon*

Tendaguru Formation, Tanzania (Jurassic).
Major finds: *Giraffatitan, Kentrosaurus, Elaphrosaurus*

Chalk rock formations in the fossil-rich White Desert, near Bahariya Oasis, Egypt.

THE FIRST RECOGNIZED AFRICAN DINOSAUR FOSSILS, BELONGING

Fossil finds

Africa has a rich fossil heritage, but so far the continent's prehistory has not been fully studied. A rush of fossil hunting in the early 20th century was interrupted by the two World Wars. It is only quite recently that paleontologists have begun again to search for signs of early life in Africa's rocks.

Lubur Sandstone Sequence, Kenya
Bones from a range of Cretaceous reptiles, including dinosaurs, have been found in the 1,640-ft (500-m) thick sequence of rocks.

Tendaguru Formation, Tanzania

Maevarano Formation, Madagascar
Incredible Cretaceous fossils include the predatory theropod *Majungasaurus* and giant "devil toad" *Beelzebufo*.

KEY

● **Dinosaur fossil site**

Bushveld Sandstone Formation, South Africa

Elliot Formation, South Africa
The rocks here date from between the Late Triassic to Early Jurassic, and are famous for many species of early dinosaur.

Spinosaurus

Spinosaurus
Remains of the giant theropod *Spinosaurus* have been found throughout the Cretaceous rocks of North Africa. The first specimen, found in 1915, was destroyed during World War II.

Upper Kirkwood Formation, South Africa

ASIA

Parrot lizard
A small dinosaur that resembled a parrot, *Psittacosaurus* came complete with a beak and quills. This plant eater was a common forest-dweller in Early Cretaceous Asia.

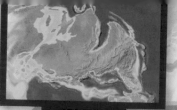

170 MYA

LAURASIA

ATLANTIC OCEAN

PACIFIC OCEAN

INDIAN OCEAN

Dominant herbivore

Shunosaurus was a very common animal in this region. In a place called Dashanpu quarry, in modern-day China, 90 percent of all the dinosaur material found belong to this sauropod.

TETHYS OCEAN

Lush forest

This habitat was rich in trees that surrounded large lakes.

Spiky tail

Shunosaurus roamed the area we now call China 170–160 million years ago. This dinosaur also possessed an interesting tail, with a small, spiked club at its end. Some experts think it was used for defense.

Low browser

The relatively short neck probably meant *Shunosaurus* foraged for plants close to the forest floor because it couldn't reach as far as its longer-necked cousins, such as *Diplodocus*.

106

TEN *SHUNOSAURUS* WERE FOUND AT JUST ONE SITE, HAVING

Shunosaurus

SHOO-noe-SORE-us

A 33-ft (10-m) long body may sound huge, but *Shunosaurus* was small compared to its giant sauropod cousins. Weighing around 3.5 tons, this dinosaur would wander through open plains and forests in search of plants to eat.

Tail weapon

A double row of 2-in (5-cm) tall spikes, called osteoderms, which lined the tail's club, might have scared off some hungry Jurassic predators.

Built to eat plants

The tall skull and long teeth of this sauropod has led some paleontologists to suggest the jaws acted like garden shears, slicing through branches.

Shunosaurus skeleton

Growing up

Leg bone analysis by scientists suggests that *Shunosaurus* continued to grow even once it had reached adulthood.

DROWNED IN A FLASH FLOOD.

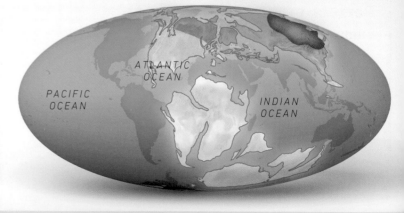

Tail quills
These structures may be related to the feathers of today's birds.

Big-brained
A large brain suggests *Psittacosaurus* may have been capable of pretty complex behaviors, such as caring for their young.

ARCTIC OCEAN

Cheek horns
Prominent horns on the cheeks grew with age, which suggests they might have been used for attracting a mate.

Family life
Hundreds of individual *Psittacosaurus* specimens have been unearthed, ranging from tiny babies to full-grown adults. One was even found next to 34 hatchlings, suggesting that this dinosaur cared for its young.

ATLANTIC OCEAN

PACIFIC OCEAN

INDIAN OCEAN

Psittacosaurus

SIT-ack-oh-SORE-us

An early relative of *Triceratops*, *Psittacosaurus* grew to 7 ft (2 m) in length and roamed the woodlands of modern-day Asia 125–100 million years ago. Based on 400 known specimens, nine species of this dinosaur have been identified.

Adaptable herbivore
Psittacosaurus species lived in a range of habitats over their 20-million-year evolution, from cool forests to arid deserts.

Large range
Fossils have been found as far north as modern-day Siberia, and south through China and Mongolia.

SOUTHEAST ASIA

TETHYS OCEAN

Early Cretaceous Asia
Modern-day India was not part of Asia at this time. It would later crash into Asia to form the Himalayas.

Perfect preservation

Study of this well-preserved specimen from China has shown that some *Psittacosaurus* species had a brown back and pale belly. This was a form of camouflage called "countershading."

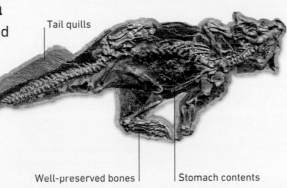

Tail quills

Well-preserved bones

Stomach contents

Parrot beak

The name *Psittacosaurus* means "parrot lizard" and refers to its parrotlike beak. The beak would have been used to slice off vegetation, which would then have been shredded by its small, sharp teeth.

Fuzzy predator

At the top of the food chain, *Yutyrannus* probably preyed upon the diverse fauna found in Early Cretaceous Asia, which included small ornithischians such as *Psittacosaurus*.

Big skull
Filled with thick, banana-shaped teeth, the 35-in (90-cm) long skull was similar to that of later tyrannosaurs.

Fuzzy coat
The feathers that covered the body were long, hairlike, and formed a dense coat.

ATLANTIC OCEAN

PACIFIC OCEAN

INDIAN OCEAN

Three-clawed hands
Both the arms and claws were proportionally larger than those seen in later tyrannosaurs and may have helped to catch prey.

Heavy tyrannosaur
Weighing around a ton, *Yutyrannus* was substantially larger than most early tyrannosaurs.

Feeding aid
The large feet might have been used to pin down carcasses while *Yutyrannus* tore chunks of meat off them with its teeth.

A DISTINCTIVE CREST RAN ALONG

Yutyrannus

you-tie-**RAN**-us

The 30-ft (9-m) long tyrannosaur *Yutyrannus* lived in Cretaceous Asia, around 125 million years ago. It is notable for the long, shaggy coat of feathers that covered its body, making it one of the largest dinosaurs known to possess plumage.

PACIFIC OCEAN

Dry seasons
While the area was generally humid and wet, there is evidence that over time water levels dropped and the region became drier.

Vast continent
The range over which *Yutyrannus* is thought to have roamed covers large parts of what is now China.

ASIA

Diverse plants
The diverse plant life, including conifer trees and various smaller plants, helped sustain a huge range of animals for *Yutyrannus* to prey upon.

Feathered tyrant
Paleontologists believe that *Yutyrannus*'s feathers—some of which grew as long as 8 in (20 cm)—may have helped regulate its temperature. With average air temperatures during this time around 50°F (10°C), feathers would have kept it warm in the winter months.

Reconstructed face of *Yutyrannus*

Long tail
As in other tyrannosaurs, the heavy tail helped with balance.

Surprise attack

A large *Yutyrannus* launches out of its hiding place and sinks its serrated teeth into the flesh of the herbivore *Beipiaosaurus*. Two *Psittacosaurus* use the commotion to escape toward the safety of the forest.

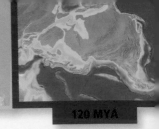

Folding wrist
The wings folded at the wrist, which prevented them from being damaged by trailing them on the ground.

Shiny plumage
Studies of pigments in fossilized *Microraptor* feathers revealed that it had shimmering black plumage. In fact, the feathers would look much like those of modern birds, such as starlings.

Powered flight
Microraptor appears to have been capable of taking off from the ground for short bursts of flight.

Mixed diet
Living around 120 million years ago, *Microraptor* had a varied diet. The fossilized stomach contents of several of these dinosaurs show that it ate small mammals, fish, and a type of extinct bird.

Tail feathers
These long feathers may have been used for display rather than flight, perhaps to attract partners.

Microraptor

my-CROW-rap-ter

One of the smallest known dinosaurs, this little predator weighed about 2 lb (1 kg) and was around 30 in (80 cm) long. *Microraptor* had four "wings" and was fully feathered, with extra-long arm and leg feathers. Its fossils have all been found in modern-day China.

Airborne
Microraptor had a wingspan of roughly 28 in (70 cm), wide enough for it to take to the air.

Preservation
There was volcanic activity across this area of eastern Asia. The volcanic ash preserved the soft tissue, such as feathers, in fossils.

Cool climate
The climate of this region of Asia was cool, with temperatures around 50°F (10°C).

ASIA

ATLANTIC OCEAN

PACIFIC OCEAN

INDIAN OCEAN

Fish trap
The teeth are serrated on one side only, which may have helped *Microraptor* to grip slippery fish.

Razor teeth
Below its upturned snout, this dinosaur's jaws were filled with sharp, meat-slicing teeth.

Killer claw
Located on the second toe of each foot, the 2.5-in (6.5-cm) claw was held off the ground, which kept it sharp. It might have been used to pin down struggling prey, while the rest of the foot provided grip.

Fossilized *Velociraptor* claw

Foldable wrist
The birdlike wrist could bend to stop long feathers from dragging on the ground.

AN UNDIGESTED PTEROSAUR BONE WAS FOUND IN THE RIBCAGE

Velociraptor

veh-loss-ih-**RAP**-tor

Of all the predatory tools used by the 6.5-ft (2-m) long *Velociraptor*, none is more famous than its "killer claws." Prowling parts of what is today Mongolia and China, this dinosaur used these deadly weapons to tackle prey.

Large eyes
Good eyesight gave *Velociraptor* an advantage when detecting small prey.

Little rain
In *Velociraptor*'s inland range, rain clouds would have been rare, creating a dry and dusty environment.

Athletic body
Velociraptor had a lean body that was built for speed and agility rather than strength.

Dry habitat
This was a dry region of ever-changing sand dunes. Water was scarce, and *Velociraptor* may have only found water in rare oases or temporary rivers.

Fine feathers
Velociraptor probably possessed extensive plumage, as remains of its close cousins have been discovered bearing feathers.

ASIA

Trapped in time
One *Velociraptor* specimen was found to have died fighting—its skeleton locked in combat with the herbivore *Protoceratops*. The wrestling dinosaurs may have been killed and buried by a collapsing sand dune.

Mongolian hunter
Living 74–70 million years ago, *Velociraptor* was a small but deadly predator. It had more than 60 teeth lining its jaws, which were more serrated on one side than the other. This helped tear through tough muscle.

Ilek Formation,
Siberia, Russia

Bostobinskaya
Formation, Kazakhstan

Xinminbao Group,
Gansu, China

A S I A

Lameta
Formation,
India

**Shemshak Group,
Kerman Province, Iran**
A diverse range of Jurassic
dinosaur footprints were
uncovered at this site.

Earth today

Fossil finds

Asia

The quality of the preservation of fossils from certain
locations in Asia is nothing short of breathtaking.
Key finds range from soft tissues, such as feathers and
skin pigments, to whole nurseries of baby dinosaurs.

Djadochta Formation, Gobi Desert, Mongolia

Yuliangze Formation, Jiliu Province, China

Amur River Region, Russia

Kitadani Formation, Fukui Province, Japan
A variety of Cretaceous dinosaur remains have been found here.

Yixian Formation, Liaoning Province, China

Nemegt Formation, Gobi Desert, Mongolia

Laijia Formation, China.
Numerous dinosaur egg fossils were uncovered here.

Dashanpu Formation, Sichuan, China
Sauropod remains dating back to the Jurassic have been found at this site.

Lufeng Formation, Yunnan, China
These early Jurassic rocks preserved many sauropodomorphs (long-necked plant eaters) and theropod species.

Sao Khua Formation, Thailand

Protoceratops

Fossils of this small ceratopsian are common in the Late Cretaceous rocks of Mongolia. It lacked the horns seen in some of its cousins, but had a large neck frill.

Major fossil sites

Bostobinskaya Formation, Kazakhstan (Cretaceous).
Major finds: *Arstanosaurus, Batyrosaurus*

Ilek Formation, Siberia, Russia (Cretaceous).
Major finds: *Sibirotitan, Psittacosaurus*

Nemegt Formation, Gobi Desert, Mongolia (Cretaceous).
Major finds: *Tarbosaurus, Avimimus, Conchoraptor, Zanabazar, Deinocheirus, Saichania, Saurolopus, Nemegtosaurus*

Djadochta Formation, Gobi Desert, Mongolia (Cretaceous).
Major finds: *Oviraptor, Citipati, Velociraptor, Byronosaurus, Plesiohadros, Protoceratops*

Amur River Region, Russia (Cretaceous).
Major find: *Kundurosaurus*

Yuliangze Formation, Jiliu Province, China (Cretaceous).
Major finds: *Charonosaurus, Wulagasaurus*

Yixian Formation, Liaoning Province, China (Cretaceous).
Major finds: *Beipiaosaurus, Microraptor, Psittacosaurus*

Xinminbao Group, Gansu, China (Cretaceous).
Major finds: *Gobititan, Equijubus, Microceratus, Archaeoceratops*

Lameta Formation, India (Cretaceous).
Major finds: *Indosuchus, Jainosaurus, Isisaurus*

Sao Khua Formation, Thailand (Cretaceous).
Major find: *Phuwiangosaurus*

This skeleton of feathered theropod *Microraptor* from the Early Cretaceous was found in Liaoning Province, China.

AUSTRALIA AND ANTARCTICA

Giant plant eater

A massively built herbivore with a uniquely shaped snout, *Muttaburrasaurus* foraged for food 100 million years ago. This dinosaur roamed a large section of the country that we call Australia today.

Small brain
Research suggests the brain was primitive compared to later, more intelligent allosaurs and tyrannosaurs.

Predator potential
Experts noted that the original *Cryolophosaurus* specimen was probably a subadult. So when fully grown, these dinosaurs were larger than 23 ft (7 m) in length and capable of tackling large prey.

Serrated teeth
Although it probably couldn't bite through bone, its sharp, bladelike teeth were perfect for tearing through flesh.

Cryolophosaurus
CRY-uh-**LOF**-uh-**SORE**-us

Early Jurassic predatory theropods didn't get much bigger than the 23-ft (7-m) long *Cryolophosaurus*. Most famous for its distinctive crest, it was Antarctica's top predator and hunted in forests 170 million years ago.

Curious crest

The small and flimsy crest of *Cryolophosaurus* was probably not used in combat, as it would have broken off too easily. Instead, it may have been a good indicator of fitness and used to attract mates.

Cryolophosaurus skull

Antarctic forest

Forested areas, particularly near the coasts, may have provided the perfect cover for *Cryolophosaurus* to hunt.

GONDWANA

Supercontinent

At this time, Africa, South America, Antarctica, and Australia were all still attached to one another, forming a huge landmass called Gondwana.

Warmer climate

Antarctica in the Early Jurassic sat around 620 miles (1,000 km) farther north than where the continent lies today. This led to warmer temperatures; however, inland areas would have been relatively cool.

Long arms

Cryolophosaurus may have used its long arms and sharp claws to grasp prey.

Fleet footed

As a lightweight predator, it was probably a fast and agile hunter.

ATLANTIC OCEAN

PACIFIC OCEAN

INDIAN OCEAN

A welcome discovery

It has been a good summer for this *Cryolophosaurus*. Making the most of the warmer temperatures and sunshine, it has found the carcass of a *Glacialisaurus* in a lake. The energy it will get from eating its meal will be invaluable, as a long, cold winter lies ahead.

Muttaburrasaurus

MOO-tah-**BUH**-ruh-**SORE**-us

This 26-ft (8-m) long herbivore is one of the better-known dinosaurs found in the fossil-poor rocks of Australia. It lived 112–100 million years ago, in the southeastern regions of the supercontinent Gondwana.

Broad skull
The wide skull anchored strong muscles to move the jaw and help chop up food.

Famous find
Fossils of the large ornithopod *Muttaburrasaurus* were first discovered in 1963, and named after the nearby town of Muttaburra in the Australian state of Queensland.

Strong beak
The sharp-edged beak sheared off leaves, which were then chewed in the animal's large cheeks.

Peculiar snout
The bones of this dinosaur's snout formed a hollow crest. Some experts think this amplified calls, while others think it was topped with an inflatable sac, as seen in some modern seals.

Inflatable sac

Male hooded seal

Cretaceous diet
Ferns and cycads were the likely diet of this herbivore.

SOME MUTTABURRASAURUS FOSSILS ARE PRESERVED

Marine burial

Though this dinosaur lived on land, the first skeleton was found in marine rocks, suggesting its body was washed out to sea.

Tough teeth

Muttaburrasaurus possessed large, widely spaced teeth that were suited to slicing up tough vegetation. This was unlike later ornithopods, which had jaws where hundreds of small teeth crowded together.

Muttaburrasaurus teeth

ATLANTIC OCEAN

PACIFIC OCEAN

INDIAN OCEAN

AUSTRALIA

Prehistoric forests

Muttaburrasaurus probably browsed in the forests that covered parts of Australia at the time.

Breaking up

In the Cretaceous, Gondwana started to break up as Australia split away from Antarctica.

Five-fingered hand

The strong, weight-bearing fingers meant *Muttaburrasaurus* was probably able to walk on all fours.

Eromanga Sea
At the time, a shallow sea covering much of Australia's inland areas housed giant marine reptiles. Today, this area around the central and northeastern part of the country is largely arid.

Eromanga Sea

AUSTRALIA

Polar forests
Evergreen trees covering the southern regions closest to the South Pole were capable of surviving cold temperatures and low light levels.

Volcanism
What is now eastern Australia would have been blanketed in magma and ash due to volcanic activity.

ANTARCTICA

Long tail
More than 70 vertebrae made up the tail, yet it was still more flexible than the tails of its larger cousins.

ATLANTIC OCEAN

PACIFIC OCEAN

INDIAN OCEAN

Sharp beak
A birdlike beak was perfect for nipping off low-lying vegetation, such as ferns and horsetails.

Agile runner
A low center of gravity and flexible tail suggest it could dart around the forest floor, perhaps to escape predators.

SOME PALEONTOLOGISTS THINK THE *LEAELLYNASAURA* BONES ARE

Excellent vision
Large eyes might have helped *Leaellynasaura* to see well in the darker winter months.

Feathered body
Featherlike structures might have kept it warm during the long, cold, and dark days.

Polar specialist
Scientists can't agree how severe winter conditions were in Early Cretaceous Australia. However, with average air temperatures ranging between 2°F (-6°C) and 59°F (15°C), some believe *Leaellynasaura* could have made burrows for winter shelter.

Dinosaur Cove
Although relatively few fossil discoveries have been made in Australia, Dinosaur Cove in southeastern Australia has yielded some important finds. These include the country's first dinosaur fossil in 1903 and *Leaellynasaura* in 1989.

Leaellynasaura
lee-**ELL**-in-ah-**SORE**-uh

A small dinosaur with one of the longest tails proportional to its body, the 8-ft (2.5-m) long *Leaellynasaura* scurried around the forests that would later become Australia. These agile herbivores would have experienced long periods of darkness because, 120–110 million years ago, this region was very close to the South Pole.

Earth today

Toolebuc Formation, Queensland, Australia

Allaru Formation, Queensland, Australia

Winton Formation, Queensland, Australia

Broome Sandstone Formation, Western Australia
The largest dinosaur footprints ever discovered were found here, measuring 5.6 ft (1.7 m) wide and belonging to a sauropod.

AUSTRALIA

Molecap Greensand Formation, Western Australia
A theropod dinosaur bone has been recovered from this site near Perth.

Fossil finds
Australasia and Antarctica

The harsh climate and geology of Australia, Antarctica, and New Zealand make it hard to find dinosaur fossils. When remains are discovered, they are often fragmentary and incomplete, so experts have difficulty concluding what animal they belonged to.

KEY

● Dinosaur fossil site

Richmond pliosaur

Measuring more than 13 ft (4 m) in length, the skeleton of this marine reptile was found in Queensland in 1990.

Snow Hill Island Formation, James Ross Island

ANTARCTICA

Lopez de Bertodano Formation, Vega Island

Hanson Formation, Mount Kirkpatrick, Transantarctic Mountains, Antarctica

Griman Creek Formation, New South Wales, Australia

Blackstone Formation, Queensland, Australia
Triassic footprints found here are some of the earliest evidence of dinosaurs in Australia.

Major fossil sites

Winton Formation, Queensland, Australia (Cretaceous).
Major finds: *Diamantinasaurus, Wintonotitan, Australovenator*

Toolebuc Formation, Queensland, Australia (Cretaceous).
Major find: *Muttaburrasaurus*

Allaru Formation, Queensland, Australia (Cretaceous).
Major finds: *Austrosaurus, Kunbarrasaurus*

Griman Creek Formation, New South Wales, Australia (Cretaceous).
Major find: *Muttaburrasaurus*

Wonthaggi Formation, Victoria, Australia (Cretaceous).
Major find: *Qantassaurus*

Chatham Islands, New Zealand (Cretaceous).
Major find: Theropods

Snow Hill Island Formation, James Ross Island, Antarctica (Cretaceous).
Major finds: *Trinisaura, Morrosaurus*

Lopez de Bertodano Formation, Vega Island, Antarctica (Cretaceous).
Major find: Hadrosaurs

Hanson Formation, Mount Kirkpatrick, Transantarctic Mountains, Antarctica (Jurassic).
Major finds: *Glacialisaurus, Cryolophosaurus*

Hawke's Bay, North Island, New Zealand
A huge 40-ft (12-m) long marine reptile, *Moanasaurus*, was found here, as well as the bones of theropods, ornithischians, and other dinosaur groups.

Wonthaggi Formation, Victoria, Australia

Eumeralla Formation, Victoria, Australia
The numerous remains uncovered here make it one of the best places in Australia to find dinosaur fossils.

Chatham Islands, New Zealand

AFTER THE DINOSAURS

Still a dangerous world
Even without *Tyrannosaurus* around, prehistoric life could still be dangerous. Here, an ancestor of Australia's red kangaroo flees from the claws of *Varanus priscus*, a giant monitor lizard.

Snake in a coal mine
Along with numerous fossil animals, including mammals, *Titanoboa* was found at a site in modern-day Colombia that is located within a working coal mine.

Surrounding sea
Colombia was once surrounded and partially covered by shallow seas.

S O U T H
A M E R I C A

Recreating a giant

Although the only fossils yet found of *Titanoboa* are skull fragments and some vertebrae, scientists have been able to build up an image of what the huge snake looked like. The sculptor Kevin Hockley created the full-sized model seen below, which shows *Titanoboa* gulping down a crocodilelike reptile.

Hungry predator
Feeding on fish and reptiles, *Titanoboa* inhabited a small, swampy region.

PACIFIC
OCEAN

Slow mover
Like modern boas, *Titanoboa* probably moved slowly, using its belly muscles in wavelike motions to crawl along.

Water dweller
Titanoboa may have spent most of its time in water, which would have helped support its weight.

Titanoboa

TIE-tan-o-BO-a

Sixty million years ago, in the part of South America that is now Colombia, hot swampy jungles were home to the biggest snake ever. *Titanoboa* was related to modern boa constrictors, but at a gigantic 40 ft (12 m) long, it far exceeded them in size.

ATLANTIC
OCEAN

PACIFIC
OCEAN

INDIAN
OCEAN

TITANOBOA WAS ESTIMATED TO BE NEARLY TWICE AS LONG AND

Forested world

When *Titanoboa* was alive, South America was covered in thick tropical forest, as were the other continents. Jungles stretched from pole to pole and global temperatures were high. Earth was in what we now call a "greenhouse" phase, perhaps because volcanic gases had warmed up the atmosphere.

Crushing power

Powerful muscles would have enabled *Titanoboa* to suffocate large prey by squeezing it in its coils.

Heavyweight

Titanoboa weighed more than 2,425 lb (1,100 kg), its body was 3 ft (1 m) wide, and its head was 16 in (40 cm) long.

Fish catcher

The slim, curved, pointed teeth suggest that *Titanoboa* caught large fish.

Massive jaws

Like nearly all snakes, *Titanoboa* could open its jaws wide enough to swallow prey whole. It had a long, broad skull with loosely hinged jaw bones.

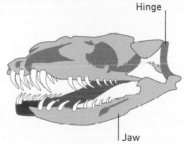

Hinge

Jaw

In a snake, a hinge joint allows the jaws to open very wide.

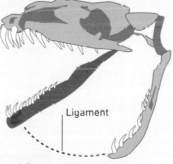

Ligament

A ligament joining the two sides of the jaws stretches as the snake opens its mouth.

Flexible neck
A bendy neck allowed *Gastornis* to look in all directions.

Tropical land
Dense, tropical forests covered most of North America during the time that *Gastornis* was alive.

Atlantic land bridge
Europe and North America were connected, enabling animals to move between the two areas via modern-day Greenland.

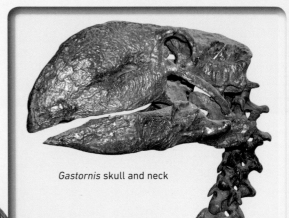

Gastornis skull and neck

Gigantic bill
Experts once believed that *Gastornis* must have used its enormous, powerful bill for tearing meat or crunching bones. It is now thought to be more likely that the bill was used for breaking branches, cracking nuts, and opening fruit.

Fur or feathers?
Gastornis is often pictured with shaggy, hairlike plumage, but it may have had normal feathers like a duck.

Walk, don't run
This hefty bird could run, but it was not built for speed. Its thick, heavy leg bones were more suited to walking.

Duck relative
Gastornis was long thought to belong to the group of birds that includes modern rails and cranes. Experts now consider it likely to have been a giant relative of ducks, geese, and swans.

European range
Gastornis ranged across western Europe, including in modern-day France, Germany, and England.

Across Asia
A single, incomplete fossil found in China has opened up the possibility that *Gastornis* may have roamed throughout Asia.

PACIFIC OCEAN

ATLANTIC OCEAN

INDIAN OCEAN

EUROPE

ASIA

Islands
High sea lea *Islands*
High sea levels at this time meant that Europe existed as a series of islands.

Plant eater
The thick-edged bill lacked the hooked tip common in meat-eating birds. This is evidence that *Gastornis* was mostly a herbivore, plucking twigs, seeds, and fruits from trees and shrubs.

Tiny wings
Gastornis had wings, but they were too small for flight.

Gastornis
Gas-**TORE**-niss

After the mass extinction event that wiped out the dinosaurs, new kinds of birds evolved. One of them, *Gastornis*, was an enormous flightless bird that lived across Europe and North America 56–40 million years ago. Standing 6.5 ft (2 m) tall, it had a deep skull and a massive bill.

HUGE FOSSIL FOOTPRINTS, THOUGHT TO BE THOSE OF GASTORNIS.

Life in water
Adapted for underwater life, the ear and skull bones of *Basilosaurus* allowed for sensitive underwater hearing.

Complex teeth
Unlike modern whales, *Basilosaurus* had teeth of several different shapes. Those in the front were simple and conical, while the teeth farther back were triangular and jagged, helping this hunter to tear up its prey.

Conical teeth

Triangular teeth

ATLANTIC OCEAN

Coasts of North America
Basilosaurus was common in the Atlantic Ocean along the warm coastal waters of the modern-day United States.

Surface predator
Studies of its jaws show that *Basilosaurus* was a predator with a very powerful bite. It mostly lived in warm, shallow seas and swam in the surface waters of North America, North Africa, Europe, and Asia.

Basilosaurus
BASS-ill-oh-SORE-us

One of the largest known animals of its time, *Basilosaurus* was a whale very unlike those of today. It had a body up to 59 ft (18 m) long and tiny hind limbs with knees, ankles, and toes. This predator hunted fish and other marine mammals 40–34 million years ago.

Long body
Basilosaurus had a long, flexible body. Early illustrations imagined it as snakelike, but this is believed to be incorrect.

BASILOSAURUS MEANS "KING LIZARD," BECAUSE THE ANIMAL WAS

EUROPE

ATLANTIC
OCEAN

PACIFIC
OCEAN

INDIAN
OCEAN

One of many
Basilosaurus lived alongside a
number of other early whales
in the Tethys Ocean.

TETHYS OCEAN

Flexible flippers
The pectoral fins of
Basilosaurus were more
flexible than those of modern
whales—both the elbow and
wrist were mobile.

**India on
the move**
At this time, India had
moved a long way across
the Indian Ocean, but had
not yet collided with Asia.

A F R I C A

Fluked tail
The tail bones of
Basilosaurus show that it had
horizontal tail flukes, like
modern whales. It swam by
moving its tail up and down.

ORIGINALLY THOUGHT TO BE A REPTILE INSTEAD OF A MAMMAL.

La Brea Tar Pits
Thousands of *Smilodon* fossils come from this site in modern-day Los Angeles, where both the cats and their prey were trapped in natural pits of sticky tar.

East to west habitat
Smilodon ranged across the area that is the United States today, from Pennsylvania in the east to California in the west.

NORTH AMERICA

Killer canines

Smilodon's giant upper canine teeth were once thought to have been used for stabbing. Experts now think *Smilodon* used them to deliver a precise killing bite to the throat of its prey.

Stumpy tail
The short tail was like that of a modern lynx or bobcat.

Sharp blades
Curved and very sharp, the upper canines could be up to 11 in (28 cm) long.

Sturdy legs
Unlike most cats, *Smilodon* was not a fast runner. Its legs were short, thick, and muscular.

SMILODON NEEDED TO OPEN ITS JAWS BY ABOUT 120 DEGREES TO

PACIFIC OCEAN
ATLANTIC OCEAN
INDIAN OCEAN

Brazilian cat
The first *Smilodon* fossil was found in Brazil in 1842.

Saber-tooth kingdom

Different kinds of saber-toothed cats lived across modern-day Africa, Europe, Asia, and North and South America from 2.5 million to 10,000 years ago. *Smilodon* was a grassland hunter, but others lived in forests and woodlands. Some were smaller than *Smilodon*, but they all seem to have used their canine teeth as their main weapon.

Smilodon skull

SOUTH AMERICA

Smilodon

SMILE-oh-don

Best known of the saber-toothed cats, *Smilodon* was also one of the largest, up to 8 ft (2.5 m) long and standing 4 ft (1.2 m) tall at the shoulder. Heavy and muscular, with huge, swordlike canine teeth, it preyed on large hoofed mammals such as camels and horses.

Mystery coat
Although *Smilodon* is often shown with this coat, scientists do not know for certain if this cat was plain or patterned.

Powerful body
This cat had very strong arms and shoulders.

Life in the south
Smilodon inhabited a vast range of the Americas, all the way down to southern Argentina.

Cave paintings

Early humans illustrated woolly mammoths on European cave walls with a shoulder hump, domed head, and shaggy coat. They are sometimes shown fighting or raising their trunk.

Coat color

Genetic studies show that woolly mammoths were probably dark or sometimes blonde.

Out of Africa

Fossils show that mammoths originated in Africa, before spreading across Asia and Europe.

Massive tusks

Huge, curved tusks could grow as long as 13 ft (4 m).

Well-known giant

Many woolly mammoths have been discovered frozen in ice with their skin and hair preserved. As a result, scientists know more about this animal than any other Ice Age animal.

WOOLLY MAMMOTHS WERE

Woolly mammoth

Mammoths were a group of elephants going back 5 million years, with giant curving tusks and teeth adapted for grazing. The most famous of them, the woolly mammoth, lived in Europe, Asia, and North America 200,000–4,000 years ago. It was a midsized mammoth, around 16 ft (5 m) long.

American invasion
The woolly mammoth used the Bering Land Bridge to move to North America 30,000 years ago.

Siberian survival
Woolly mammoths survived in Wrangel Island until 4,000 years ago, when the area was free of the thick ice sheets that had existed before.

ATLANTIC OCEAN

PACIFIC OCEAN

INDIAN OCEAN

Powerful trunk
The strong, flexible trunk was covered in fur.

Frozen young
Among the most famous woolly mammoth specimens are the young that became trapped in mud and frozen in icy-cold ground. One example is Lyuba, a 1-month-old female unearthed in the Russian Arctic who was discovered in 2007.

Leg fur
Long hair grew down to the toes and kept the feet warm.

Hunting in the grasslands

Unlike some other mammoths that lived in warm habitats, woolly mammoths were cold-climate specialists. Evidence from tools, damaged bones, and ancient art shows that humans hunted this 9.8-ft (3-m) tall shaggy elephant everywhere it roamed.

Varanus priscus
vah-**RAN**-us **PRISS**-cuss

Between 1.6 million and 50,000 years ago, what is known as Australia today was home to many spectacularly gigantic animals. Among these was the 20-ft (6-m) long monitor lizard *Varanus priscus*, originally known by the name *Megalania*.

Bony crest
Unlike other monitor lizards, *Varanus priscus* had a raised bony crest on the top of its skull.

Plain or patterned
The lizard's scaly skin could have been plain or boldly marked with spots and stripes.

Toxic bite
The jaws probably had deadly venom glands.

Giant monitor lizard
Varanus priscus probably resembled the monitor lizards of today—large, long-necked predators. Its huge size meant that it could tackle big prey, such as the giant kangaroos and bear-sized relatives of wombats that shared its habitat.

ESTIMATED TO WEIGH 4,190 LB

Weighty tail
Some experts think that *Varanus priscus* had a shorter, chunkier tail than monitor lizards today.

Large landmass
During the Pleistocene, sea levels were lower than today, meaning Australia was bigger and connected by land to New Guinea.

Shared habitat
Before the species died out, *Varanus priscus* was thought to have briefly lived alongside Australia's first human settlers.

AUSTRALIA

Big claws
Long, curved claws tipped the fingers and toes and would have delivered raking wounds on the bodies of prey.

A wide range
Fossils of *Varanus priscus* have been found right across the eastern half of Australia, from Cape York Peninsula in the north to Melbourne in the south.

PACIFIC OCEAN

ATLANTIC OCEAN

INDIAN OCEAN

Reptile relatives
The largest lizard species alive today—the Komodo dragon—roamed alongside *Varanus priscus* in prehistoric Australia. Today, Komodo dragons are restricted to just a few Indonesian islands, but would have previously occupied a much larger range.

[1,900 KG], VARANUS PRISCUS IS THE BIGGEST EVER KNOWN LAND LIZARD.

147

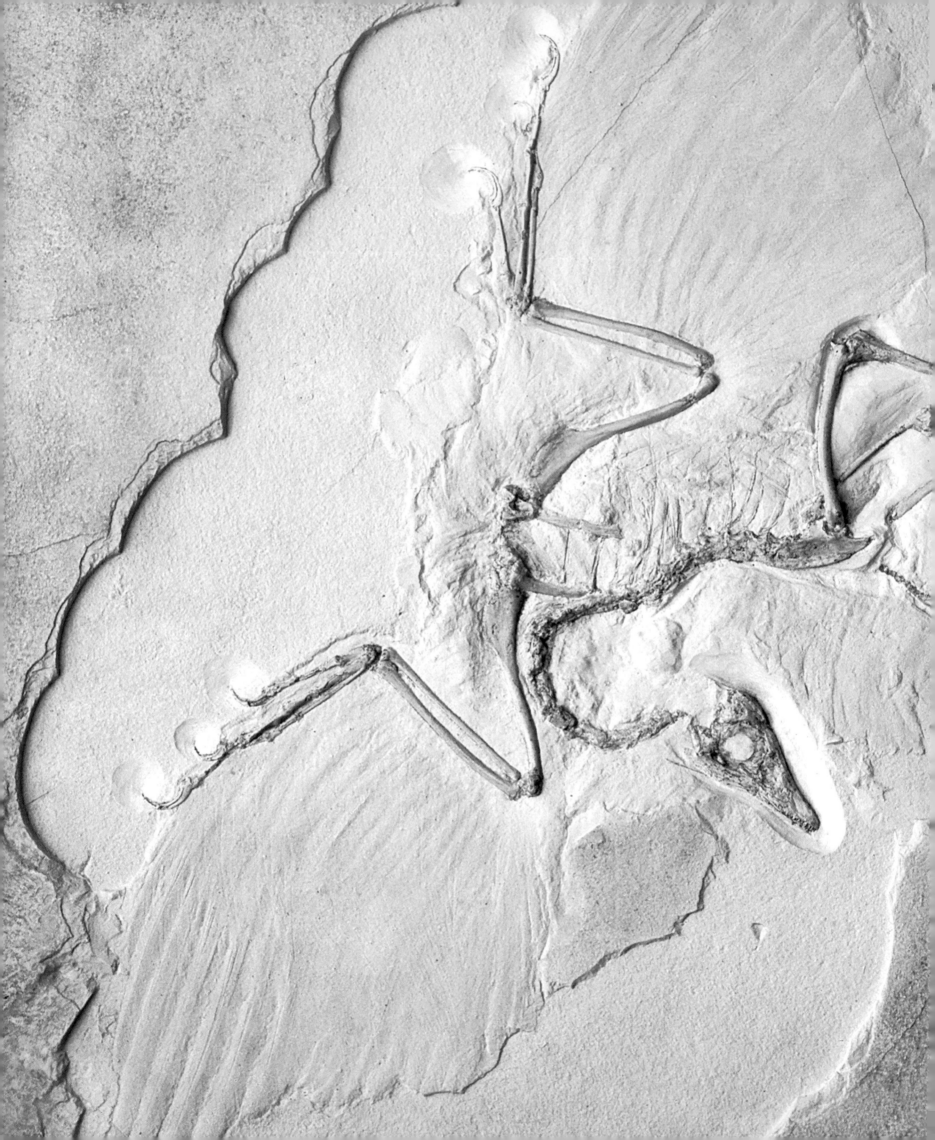

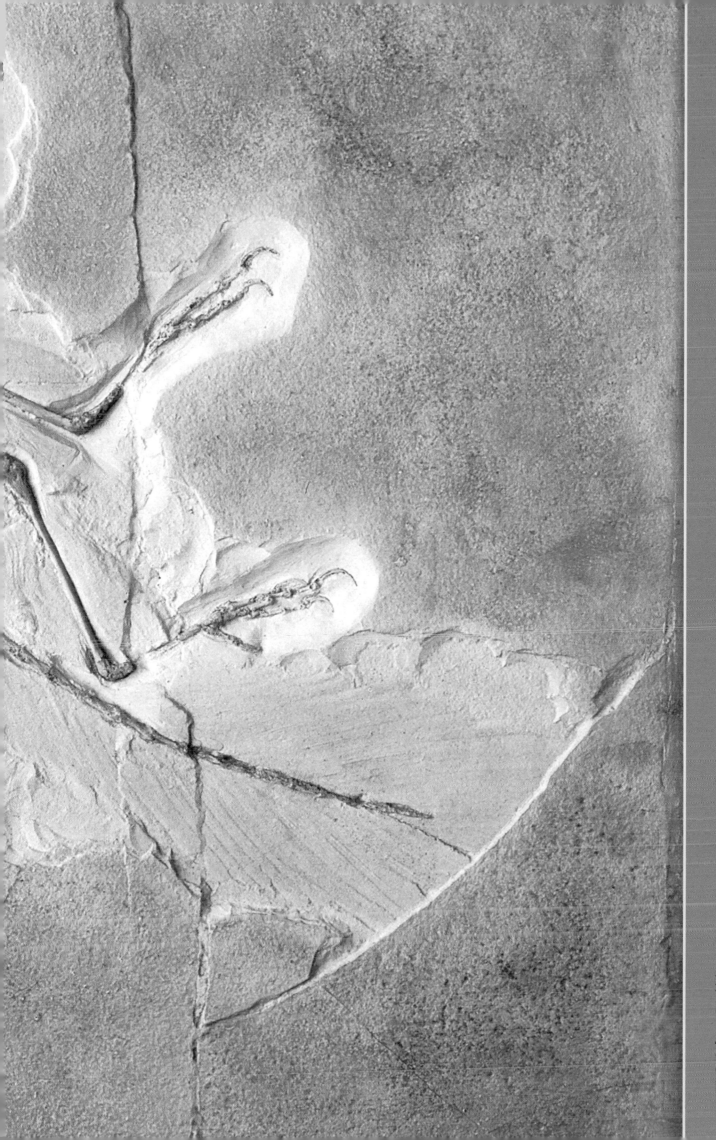

REFERENCE

Remarkable specimen
The impressions of feathers can be clearly seen in this beautifully preserved *Archaeopteryx* fossil. With every new find, experts discover more about the prehistoric world.

Fossilization

We know a lot about ancient dinosaurs, mammoths, and other extinct animals thanks to the remains we call fossils. But how do the remnants of a once-living plant, animal, or other organism become a fossil? The process requires a very specific set of conditions.

A slow process

Fossilization is a gradual process. Bones, leaves, and other remains can take thousands or millions of years to become fossilized. These four stages show how a dinosaur fossil forms, from the animal's death and preservation to its eventual discovery.

Rising oceans
Changes in sea levels can result in areas that were once dry land to become flooded by seawater.

Fossilized flora
Complete trees only become fossils under unusual circumstances, but leaves, seeds, cones, and fruit are more often preserved.

Violent lives
Some dinosaurs, even this *Tyrannosaurus*, may have been killed by other predators, only for their fossils to be discovered millions of years later.

Safe skeleton
Still conditions and few scavengers make some lakes and seas the ideal place for fossils to form.

Sediment builds
New layers of sediment constantly build up on seafloors, causing new fossils to form.

Sunken remains
A dead creature in the water will eventually sink to the bottom and may become buried in the sediment.

Uncovering the past
Millions of fossils await discovery. Every year, fossil hunters and paleontologists uncover many more.

Recently formed soft layers of sand and mud

Compressed, hardened sediment layers

Old, flattened rock layers

Death and decay
When an animal dies, its remains are usually eaten by scavengers. Some animals, however, end up in places where they become preserved, such as in a lake or ocean.

Buried in mud
If the remains are quickly buried by sand or mud, they can be preserved from scavengers. Most fossils form on lakebeds and seafloors.

Time passes
More sediment piles on top as time passes. Millions of years later, rising sea levels flood the area with sea water. The remains flatten and harden into fossils.

Fossil discovery
Layers of rock move and are worn away as continents shift and water and wind erode the land. Some fossils eventually become exposed.

Fossil types

Fossils form in several different ways. Many fossils are the hard parts of animals or plants that have been buried, preserved, and turned to stone. More rarely, the soft parts can be preserved. Sometimes, the impressions that animal feet or shells have made in the ground may become fossilized.

Soft parts
Dead animals can be buried so quickly that scavengers do not destroy the soft parts. This skin of this coelacanth fossil is visible. In some fossils, even muscles and organs remain.

Tough remains
The most familiar fossils are of hard remains. These include the preserved bones and teeth of dinosaurs such as this *Triceratops*, mammals, and the tough outer shells of other creatures like mollusks.

Stuck in amber
Trees release a sticky liquid resin that fossilizes into amber. This substance is capable of preserving insects, such as this fly. Fruit, hair, and feathers can also be preserved in amber.

Trace fossils
Animals often leave traces of their activity on sand, soil, or mud. If covered quickly by sediment, these impressions can be fossilized. Here, we can see dinosaur footprints in the Morrison Formation, Colorado.

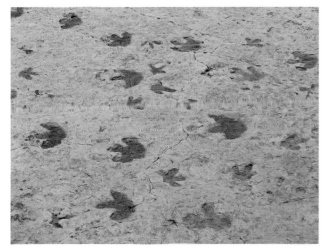

Mold and cast
This trilobite (an ancient sea creature) was buried in mud that turned to rock, preserving a mold of the animal's shape. Over time, more mud filled the mold and hardened to create a cast with the same shape as the trilobite.

Early fossils and hunters

People have found fossils since the beginning of human existence, although they did not always understand what they were. It was not until the 18th century that experts realized fossils were the remains of ancient living things.

Mary Anning

One of the most important early fossil collectors was Mary Anning of Lyme Regis in southern England. In the early 19th century, Anning discovered the first complete fossil remains of the marine reptiles called plesiosaurs and ichthyosaurs, as well as the first pterosaur. She wrote about her findings to the leading experts of the day.

Pioneering scientist
Mainly self-taught, Anning kept detailed notes about her remarkable discoveries. She also sold fossils to make a living.

Unknown objects

Before paleontologists started to study fossils, people struggled to explain what they were and where they came from. Some people thought they were plants or animals that had been turned instantly to stone. Others created stories about how they were formed. The Ancient Chinese, for example, thought that dinosaur fossils were the bones of dragons.

Devil's toenails
The extinct, thick-shelled oyster *Gryphaea* is commonly called Devil's toenails because of its ridged, ugly appearance.

Finding fossils

Our knowledge of dinosaurs and other prehistoric animals has grown with the discovery of fossils. From their finds, scientists can piece together a fossilized animal to learn about its appearance. However, early attempts to do this were based on incomplete fossils and resulted in mistakes. For example, it took decades before experts confirmed that *Velociraptor* had feathers.

The first paleontologists

The earliest paleontologists of the 17th and 18th centuries were confronted with new kinds of animals unlike anything they had seen before. They already had studied the anatomy and biology of living animals, which helped them to understand the fossils they were examining.

Georges Cuvier
Known as the "father of paleontology," French naturalist Georges Cuvier was an expert on animal anatomy and an important early expert in interpreting the remains of fossils.

Bone wars

During the late 19th century, people rushed to discover new fossils, especially those of the giant dinosaurs, and have them shipped to museums. In the United States, rival teams led by the scientists Othniel Marsh (standing in the middle, above) and Edward Cope raced to get to new sites first. This period is known as the "Bone Wars."

Modern techniques

Advances in technology have allowed experts today to piece together fossils using computers. Information from X-rays and Computerized Tomography (CT) scans is combined to build up images of the insides of fossils. As a result, paleontologists have a greater understanding of ancient animal anatomy and biology. Once a digital model exists, experts can examine the fossil without the need to handle the physical object.

Computer modeling
Fossils can now be moved around and examined in digital space rather than in the real world. This is especially useful for large, heavy fossils. This researcher is creating a digital image of a dinosaur's foot and claw.

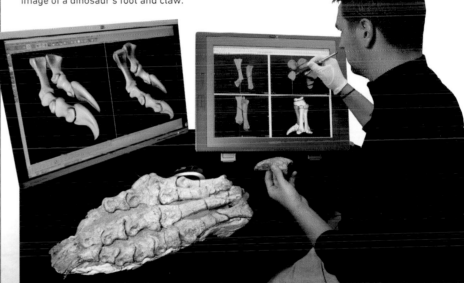

Dinosaur dig
The techniques used to take fossils out of the ground have not changed much over the years. Paleontologists require great skill and strong tools to dig up fossils. Here, two experts painstakingly unearth fossils of a prehistoric elephant in Indonesia.

Mass extinctions

On five occasions, major disasters have caused large numbers of living things to disappear entirely, including whole groups of plants and animals. These disasters are called mass extinction events. Their causes vary, from dramatic climate change to the impact of a comet, or a combination of factors.

End Ordovician

One of the most devastating mass extinction events was at the end of the Ordovician, about 443 million years ago. Around 85 percent of all ocean-dwelling animals became extinct, including crustaceanlike trilobites. The main cause of this event was probably a sudden cooling of the planet, which resulted in a huge drop in sea levels and a loss of coastal habitats.

Echinarachnius
Some ocean animals, such as this modern sea urchin, evolved in the Ordovician and survived.

End Permian

The largest mass extinction event of all happened 252 million years ago at the end of the Permian. Around 96 percent of animal species died out. The event was so catastrophic that it has been called "The Great Dying." In the seas, many invertebrate groups disappeared. On land, insect and vertebrate groups also became extinct. The cause of the event was probably the release of massive quantities of basalt and volcanic gases in modern-day Siberia.

Xenacanthus
The Permian extinction was devastating. The sharklike *Xenacanthus* was one of the few species to survive.

End Devonian

The Devonian mass extinction occurred around 358 million years ago. This extreme extinction event led to the loss of 70–80 percent of the world's animal species. Its cause is uncertain, but some possible explanations include changing sea levels, a cooling climate, and the impact of a comet.

Pterichthyodes
Numerous fish were affected by this extinction. *Pterichthyodes* is a member of the extinct group called placoderms.

Oxynoticeras
In the oceans, shelled ammonites became extinct during this period. Ammonite shells are among the most abundant of Mesozoic fossils, and hundreds of species are known.

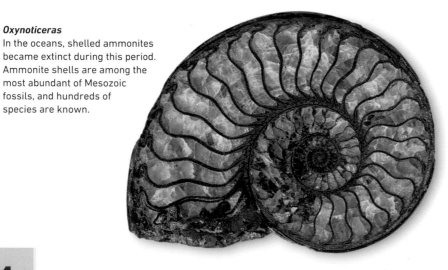

End Cretaceous

The most famous extinction happened 65.5 million years ago at the end of the Cretaceous. Because the symbol for Cretaceous is K and the symbol for the following Paleogene is Pg, the event is often called the K-Pg event. About 80 percent of animal species died out, including marine invertebrates and all dinosaurs except birds. The impact of an asteroid or comet was probably the main reason for the extinction, but changing climates caused by volcanic gas may have also contributed.

End Triassic

Around 201 million years ago, the end of the Triassic was marked by another mass extinction event. Around half of all animals died out, including giant amphibians, reef-building invertebrates, and many mollusks and marine reptiles. This extinction involved two or three episodes that happened over 18 million years. Major changes in climate—both rapid warming and cooling—is thought to be the main factor behind the extinction. This dangerous climatic pattern was most likely caused by high volcanic activity creating an increase in the release of volcanic gases. The extinction of several major reptile groups probably allowed dinosaurs to rise to dominance in the Jurassic.

Plateosaurus
Several groups of dinosaurs such as primitive sauropodomorphs, which includes *Plateosaurus*, were badly affected by the extinction.

Current extinction

We are in the early stages of a sixth mass extinction. This time, it is not geological events or rocks from space that are killing things, but humans. We are destroying wild space, polluting landscapes, changing the climate, and eating living things into extinction. Unless changes are made, huge numbers of living things will disappear forever.

Battered Earth
Giant rocks from space have collided with Earth on many occasions, sometimes with catastrophic effect. 65.5 million years ago, an object 6.2 miles (10 km) wide crashed into the Gulf of Mexico, causing a huge explosion.

Glossary

Ammonite
An extinct marine mollusk with a coiled shell and long tentacles.

Amphibian
A vertebrate animal that emerges from an egg as a tadpole and lives in water before changing into an air-breathing adult, such as a frog or a newt. Amphibians can live both on land and in water.

Ankylosaurid
A type of ankylosaur with a bony tail club that the animal used as a weapon.

Ankylosaurs
A group of dinosaurs that have armored bodies covered in bony plates.

Archosaurs
A group of reptiles that included dinosaurs, as well as the extinct relatives of crocodiles and alligators and pterosaurs. Today, the group includes modern crocodilians and birds.

Arid
Having little or no rainfall. Often used to describe a very dry environment.

Azhdarchids
A group of huge pterosaurs, common in the Late Cretaceous.

Binocular vision
The ability to see an object with two eyes, as humans do. Like us, an animal with binocular vision can see in 3-D.

Biped
An animal that moves on two legs.

Browse
To feed on the leaves of trees and shrubs.

Cambrian
A period in the Paleozoic Era that began 541 million years ago and ended 485 million years ago.

Carboniferous
A period in the Paleozoic Era that began 358 million years ago and ended 298 million years ago.

Carnivore
An animal that eats meat.

Cenozoic Era
The era that followed the Mesozoic, or the "age of the dinosaurs," which started 66 million years ago and continues in the present day.

Ceratopsians
A group of plant-eating dinosaurs, including *Triceratops*, that often had horns on their heads or bony frills at the back of the skull.

Conifer
A type of tree, often evergreen, with small, tough, needlelike leaves.

Cretaceous
A period of the Mesozoic Era that began 145 million years ago and ended 66 million years ago.

Crocodilian
An archosaur in the same group as modern crocodiles, alligators, caimans, and gharials, as well as their closest extinct relatives.

Crurotarsans
A group of reptiles that includes the crocodilians, as well as their extinct relatives.

Cycad
A type of tropical plant that has a broad crown of leaves and looks like, but is not related to, palm trees.

Dental battery
The arrangement of small, interlocking teeth, seen in some herbivorous dinosaurs that helped grind up tough plant matter.

Devonian
A period in the Paleozoic Era that began 419 million years ago and ended 358 million years ago.

Display
Behavior by an animal to pass on information to another. Display is commonly used in courtship or to ward off intruders. For example, *Cryolophosaurus*'s crest may have been used to attract potential mates.

Ecosystem
A community of living organisms that interact with each other and with their surrounding environment in a particular way.

Environment
The natural surroundings of an animal or a plant.

Era
A long span of geological time, such as the Mesozoic, that marks a particular division in the history of life. Eras are often made up of several shorter divisions of time called periods.

Evolution
The process by which animals and plants gradually change over time.

Extinction
The permanent dying out of a species, leaving no remaining individuals anywhere on Earth. Sometimes, several species or groups have become extinct at the same time.

Fern
A primitive type of nonflowering plant with leafy fronds and long stems that grows in damp places.

Flightless
Lacking the ability to fly. The term is used for animals belonging to a group of birds or insects in which the majority of species are capable of flight.

Floodplain
A flat area beside a river where sediment, carried by the water, has been deposited during high tides or seasonal floods.

Fossil
The preserved remains or traces of a prehistoric animal or plant that has been rapidly buried and turned to stone. Trace fossils can include tracks and footprints, nests, and droppings.

Fossilization
The process by which living plants or animals turn into fossils.

Ginkgo
A tall, nonflowering tree with semicircular leaves.

Hadrosaurs
A group of plant-eating dinosaurs that evolved complex sets of teeth, called dental batteries, especially adapted for browsing.

Herbivore
An animal that eats only plants.

Heterodont
Describing an animal that possesses two or more differently shaped sets of teeth in its jaws, such as sharp teeth for cutting and molars for chewing.

Horsetail
An ancient, water-loving plant that dates back to the Devonian period. It has an upright stem and thin leaves and produces spores instead of seeds.

Ichthyosaur
A prehistoric marine reptile that resembled a modern dolphin.

Jurassic
A period of the Mesozoic Era when dinosaurs dominated the land. It began 201 million years ago and ended 145 million years ago.

Keratin
A tough, fibrous protein that makes up hair, claws, horns, scales, and feathers.

Lagoon
A shallow body of salty water, often separated from the ocean by a coral reef.

Marginocephalians
A group of dinosaurs that included horned animals such as *Triceratops* and the massively thick-skulled *Pachycephalosaurus*.

Marine reptile
A reptile that lives in the ocean. The term also refers to plesiosaurs, ichthyosaurs, and mosasaurs, many of which became extinct at the end of the Cretaceous.

Mass extinction
An event or series of events that causes many types of life to die out within a short geological timespan.

Mesozoic Era
An era that spans from the Triassic, 252 million years ago, to the Cretaceous, 66 million years ago. It is sometimes referred to as the "age of the dinosaurs."

Mosasaurs
A group of large to gigantic ocean-going lizards that lived in oceans worldwide during the Cretaceous. They had paddles, tail-fins, and scaly bodies.

Nodosaurid
A type of ankylosaur that was covered in spikes and had bony shields over its hips, but did not have the tail club typical of the ankylosaurid group.

Omnivore
An animal that eats both plants and meat.

Optic lobes
Parts of the brain that process what an animal sees, such as shapes.

Ordovician
A period in the Paleozoic Era that began 485 million years ago and ended 443 million years ago.

Organism
A living thing.

Ornithischian
Belonging to one of the two major groups of dinosaurs. They are also known as "bird-hipped" dinosaurs.

Ornithomimosaurs
A group of dinosaurs that looked similar to modern ostriches and were adapted for running. Ornithomimosaurs possessed a beak, and most were toothless.

Ornithopods
A group of ornithischian (bird-hipped) dinosaurs that have birdlike feet. They include *Iguanodon* and the hadrosaurs.

Osteoderms
Bony plates embedded in the skin, making up the armor of some dinosaurs, including *Ankylosaurus*, and seen in modern animals such as crocodiles and alligators.

Pachycephalosaurs
A group of herbivorous dinosaurs with thick, domed skulls.

Paleogene
A period of the Cenozoic Era, starting 66 million years ago and ending 23 million years ago.

Paleontologist
A scientist who studies fossils and looks for evidence of ancient life.

Paleozoic
The era that came before the "age of the dinosaurs," starting 541 million years ago and ending 252 million years ago.

Pangea
A supercontinent made up of all of Earth's land surfaces joined together. It had formed by the Late Paleozoic Era.

Period
A unit of geological time that is part of an era.

Permian
A period in the Paleozoic Era that began 298 million years ago and ended 252 million years ago.

Plesiosaurs
A group of prehistoric marine reptiles that lived during the Mesozoic Era. All plesiosaurs had four winglike paddles and a short tail. Many had long, flexible necks, while others had short necks and long jaws.

Precambrian
A huge span of time that came before the Paleozoic Era and includes the Hadean, Archean, and Proterozoic periods. It started at the creation of Earth, 4.6 billion years ago, and ended at the Cambrian, 541 million years ago.

Predator
An animal that hunts and eats other animals.

Prey
An animal that is hunted as food by another animal.

Prosauropod
A commonly used name for one of several species of early, long-necked, plant-eating dinosaurs. The prosauropods did not form a true scientific group.

Pterosaurs
The family of flying reptiles found throughout the Mesozoic Era.

Quadruped
An animal that moves around on all four limbs.

Rauisuchians
A group of meat-eating archosaurs that moved on four legs and were mostly very large. They were the leading predators of the Triassic.

Reptiles
A group of animals that include turtles, lizards, crocodiles, snakes, dinosaurs, and pterosaurs.

Saurischian
Belonging to one of the two major groups of dinosaurs. Saurischians are often referred to as "lizard-hipped" dinosaurs.

Sauropod
The group of mostly gigantic, four-legged, long-necked dinosaurs that includes *Diplodocus* and *Brachiosaurus*. They evolved from the earlier sauropodomorphs known as prosauropods.

Sauropodomorphs
The large group of saurischian dinosaurs that includes the prosauropods and sauropods.

Scavenger
An animal that lives on the remains of dead animals and other scraps.

Sclerotic ring
A ring of bone embedded in the eyeball of some vertebrate animals that supports the eye.

Silurian
A period in the Paleozoic Era that began 443 million years ago and ended 419 million years ago.

Spatulate
Having a broad, flat end. The term is often used to describe the teeth of herbivorous animals.

Species
A particular type of organism that is able to breed with other individuals of the same kind.

Stegosaurs
A group of dinosaurs that often possessed broad plates or spines along their backs and tails.

Supercontinent
A gigantic landmass made up of several continents that have collided together.

Territory
The region of an animal's habitat that it defends from rival animals, usually of its own kind.

Tetrapod
A vertebrate animal with four limbs, or descends from ancestors that had four limbs. Today's snakes and whales are tetrapods.

Theropod
One of the two major groups of saurischian (lizard-hipped) dinosaurs. Theropods are often carnivorous and bipedal, and include modern-day birds.

Thyreophorans
A group of dinosaurs that includes the armored ankylosaurs and stegosaurs.

Titanosaurs
A group of sauropod dinosaurs that were often of immense size. Some of the titanosaurs were the largest land animals ever to exist.

Triassic
A period of the Mesozoic Era that began 252 million years ago and ended 201 million years ago.

Tyrannosaurids
A group of large, meat-eating theropods that included *Tyrannosaurus rex*. Predators of this kind evolved in the Late Cretaceous and had huge jaws adapted for bone-crunching bites.

Vegetation
Plant material.

Vertebrae
The bones forming the backbone of a vertebrate animal.

Vertebrate
An animal—such as a dinosaur, mammal, bird, and fish—with a backbone made up of vertebrae.

Index

Acknowledgments

Dorling Kindersley would like to thank:
Sarah Edwards, Vicky Richards, and
Jenny Sich for editorial assistance;
Kit Lane and Shahid Mahmood for design
assistance; Elizabeth Wise for the index;
Caroline Stamps for proofreading.

Smithsonian Enterprises:
Kealy Gordon, Product Development
Manager; Ellen Nanney, Senior Manager,
Licensed Publishing; Jill Corcoran,
Director, Licensed Publishing; Brigid
Ferraro, Vice President, Consumer
and Education Products; Carol LeBlanc,
Senior Vice President, Consumer
and Education Products

Reviewer for the Smithsonian:
Matthew T. Miller, Museum Technician
(Collections Volunteer Manager),
Department of Paleobiology, National
Museum of Natural History

**The publisher would like to thank the
following for their kind permission
to reproduce their photographs:**
(Key: a-above; b-below/bottom; c-centre;
f-far; l-left; r-right; t-top)

11 Alamy Stock Photo: Angela DeCenzo
(bc). **Science Photo Library:** Chris Butler
(br). **13 Getty Images:** Albert Lleal / Minden
Pictures (ca). **Science Photo Library:** Jaime
Chirinos (cr). **18 Dorling Kindersley:** James
Kuether (cl). **22–147 plants by Xfrog,
www.xfrog.com:** (Trees, bushes on maps).
22 Dorling Kindersley: State Museum
of Nature, Stuttgart (bc). **25 Dorling
Kindersley:** Senckenberg Nature Museum,
Frankfurt (cr). **28 Alamy Stock Photo:** age
fotostock (bl). **29 123RF.com:** Dave Willman
/ dcwcreations (br). **30 Getty Images:**
Francesco Tomasinelli / AGF / UIG (cla).
31 iStockphoto.com: ivan-96 (cr).
32 Science Photo Library: Natural History
Museum, London (bl). **36 Dorling
Kindersley:** Natural History Museum,
London (clb). **38 Dorling Kindersley:** Royal

Tyrrell Museum of Palaeontology, Alberta,
Canada (cla). **41 Dorling Kindersley:** The
American Museum of Natural History (crb).
Dreamstime.com: Peter.wey (br).
44 Dorling Kindersley: Natural History
Museum, London (clb). **46 Dorling
Kindersley:** Oxford Museum of Natural
History (cr). **49 Alamy Stock Photo:** William
Mullins (br). **52 Science Photo Library:**
Millard H. Sharp (bl). **54 Getty Images:** Eitan
Abramovich / AFP (clb). **56 Getty Images:**
Independent Picture Service / UIG (clb).
60 Alamy Stock Photo: Rebecca Jackrel
(br). **62 www.skullsunlimited.com:** (bl).
63 Depositphotos Inc: AndreAnita (br).
65 Getty Images: Photograph by Michael
Schwab (cr). **68 Dorling Kindersley:** (tl).
72 Alamy Stock Photo: World History
Archive (cla). **74 Alamy Stock Photo:** John
MacTavish (br). **75 Getty Images:** Robert
Clark / National Geographic (br). **76 Alamy
Stock Photo:** The Natural History Museum
(bl). **79 Alamy Stock Photo:** Arco Images
GmbH (bl). **Dorling Kindersley:** Natural
History Museum, London (br). **81 The
Trustees of the Natural History Museum,
London:** (br). **82 www.eofauna.com:** (clb).
83 Alamy Stock Photo: Biosphoto (bc).
86–87 Studio 252MYA: Julio Lacerda.
89 Getty Images: Olaf Kruger (cra).
92 Alamy Stock Photo: The Bookworm
Collection (bl). **94 123RF.com:** Vladimir
Blinov / vblinov (b). **Science Photo Library:**
Mauricio Anton (bl). **96 Reuters:** Reinhard
Krause (br). **97 123RF.com:** Barisic Zaklina
(crb). **98 Alamy Stock Photo:** World History
Archive (cl). **100–101 Davide Bonadonna**.
102 Alamy Stock Photo: Mike P Shepherd
(br). **107 Alamy Stock Photo:** The Natural
History Museum (bl). **109 Dorling
Kindersley:** Natural History Museum,
London (br); Senckenberg Gesellshaft Fuer
Naturforschugn Museum (bc). **111 Alamy
Stock Photo:** Goran Bogicevic (br).
114 Alamy Stock Photo: Lou-Foto (cl).
116 Science Photo Library: Dirk Wiersma
(br). **117 Louie Psihoyos ©psihoyos.com:**
(br). **119 Alamy Stock Photo:** Martin Shields

(br). **123 Getty Images:** Kazuhiro Nogi /
AFP (cra). **126 Getty Images:** Morales (bl).
127 Alamy Stock Photo: Richard Cummins
(cra). **129 Science Photo Library:** Peter
Menzel (crb). **134 Getty Images:** Michael
Loccisano (cl). **137 Richtr Jan:** (crb).
138 Alamy Stock Photo: Roland Bouvier
(clb). **141 Alamy Stock Photo:** Scott
Camazine (cra). **142 Alamy Stock Photo:**
Granger Historical Picture Archive (cl).
143 Rex by Shutterstock: Matt Dunham /
AP (bc). **147 123RF.com:** Andrey Gudkov
(br). **151 123RF.com:** Camilo Maranchón
García (bl); W. Scott McGill (cb). **Dorling
Kindersley:** Natural History Museum,
London (tr); Royal Tyrrell Museum of
Palaeontology, Alberta, Canada (c); Natural
History Museum (br). **152 Alamy Stock
Photo:** Pictorial Press Ltd (cra). **Getty
Images:** James Thompson / Underwood
Archives (bl). **152–153 Alamy Stock Photo:**
Reynold Sumayku (b). **153 Alamy Stock
Photo:** Science History Images (tl). **Science
Photo Library:** Pascal Goetgheluck (cr).
154–155 Science Photo Library: Mark
Garlick (b). **155 123RF.com:** Vladimir
Salman (cra)

All other images © Dorling Kindersley
For further information see:
www.dkimages.com